Simply Indispensable

Simply Indispensable

An Action Guide for School Librarians

Janice Gilmore-See

LIBRARIES UNLIMITED

AN IMPRINT OF ABC-CLIO, LLC
Santa Barbara, California • Denver, Colorado • Oxford, England

Library of Congress Cataloging-in-Publication Data

Gilmore-See, Janice.
    Simply indispensable : an action guide for school librarians / Janice Gilmore-See.
        p. cm.
    Includes bibliographical references and index.
    ISBN 978-1-59158-799-6 (acid-free paper)—ISBN 978-1-59158-800-9 (ebook)
    1. School libraries—United States—Administration. I. Title.
    Z675.S3G5525 2010
    025.1'978—dc22   2010012798

ISBN: 978-1-59158-799-6
EISBN: 978-1-59158-800-9

14 13 12 11 10   1 2 3 4 5

This book is also available on the World Wide Web as an e-book.
Visit http://www.abc-clio.com for details.

Libraries Unlimited
An Imprint of ABC-CLIO, LLC

ABC-CLIO, LLC
130 Cremona Drive, P.O. Box 1911
Santa Barbara, California 93116-1911

This book is printed on acid-free paper ∞

Manufactured in the United States of America

Contents

Acknowledgments

Thank you to my parents, Charlyn, Steve, and Tom, for a lifetime of support and encouragement, for passing on the writer's gene to me, and for listening to my travails; to my husband, Patrick, and our children Brandon, Chris, Dillon, and Amber, for cleaning the house and keeping things going; to Jane Lofton, my California School Library Association mentor; to the library media techs and teachers at La Mesa-Spring Valley School District; to my editor, Blanche Woolls, without whom this would have been impossible; and to Franki Corless, for finding the perfect title for this book.

Introduction

What Does It Mean to Be Simply Indispensable?

Being indispensable means that even in times of budget cuts, the library program is not considered a potential target. Being indispensable means you have a front line of administrators, teachers, students, parents, and a community who protect their school library from all threats coming from both inside and outside, from above and all around.

In an article examining graduating high school students' lack of readiness for college, Rettig, an academic librarian writing while president of the American Library Association, points out the importance of state certified school librarians.

> "Librarians are teachers just as much as those assigned to classrooms (indeed, 90 percent of a school librarian's day is spent teaching children), and they collaborate with other teachers to give students rich learning experiences. Other teachers, hard-pressed to meet their own responsibilities, cannot keep up with all of the books, videos, and Web sites that would be beneficial to students. They depend on their school's librarian to expose children to good information and to ensure that high-school graduates are information literate—and so, in turn, do college professors and librarians."[1]

So how do we do this when we have so many other tasks facing us daily?

Our Daily Challenges

Whether working alone or as part of a small team, school librarians are generalists—meaning they usually do it all. The school librarian's job is full of variety and can be intellectually challenging and emotionally rewarding. It can also be overwhelming! Most school libraries have a very small staff. Elementary schools may have only one part-time person working in the library, and increasingly this is a paraprofessional. High schools, while more likely to have a certified teacher-librarian, may have several thousand students to serve.

Typical middle and high school duties include answering reference questions, helping students with recalcitrant computers, selecting and purchasing new books for the collection, cataloging new materials, helping a patron find a book, editing the column for the parent newsletter, writing a grant, updating the library Web site, fixing the copy machine, collaborating with teachers, co-teaching lessons, setting up bookmarks for a research topic that a teacher requested, preparing a budget for an upcoming event, and checking materials out to patrons at the circulation desk, often all in one day.

At an elementary school, an average day might include reading stories to primary students, teaching information literacy skills to visiting classes, providing reading instruction support or guiding literature circles for advanced readers, checking in and shelving several hundred books, assisting students with finding and checking out materials, answering e-mails from teachers, checking out textbooks to new students, filling interlibrary loan requests, running reading incentive reports (usually accelerated reader or reading counts), sending out overdue notices, and changing the library bulletin board to promote a theme or newly acquired materials.

With all of this activity claiming the attention and energy of the school librarian, it is not surprising that librarians often overlook or avoid interactions with others that could potentially add to their already frenetic pace. Librarians may be forced to make tough decisions or prioritize how they will spend their time.

- Which is more important, attending the staff meeting or keeping the library open after school for parents and students?
- How much time should the school librarian be willing to spend if they're not being paid for it? For example, the library may not be expected to remain open on back-to-school night or open house, but this may be the only time the school librarian can connect with parents.
- Are PTA and school site council meetings held at inconvenient times?
- Are certified school librarians or classified library workers feeling pressure from their unions or coworkers? It is not uncommon for union leaders to discourage their members from doing any activity that they aren't paid to do. This is meant to keep administrators from taking advantage of employees, and certainly that is admirable. An unfortunate side effect of this policy, however, is that employees who want to be more involved are afraid to do so.

Librarians in very busy library media centers may get a rude shock when they are informed they are being cut because of budget difficulties. They have been busy in the library and haven't been able to be a part of the school, where they could've been making connections with teachers, parents, and students. They are surprised and unprepared to showcase the importance of the library program they built to support the mission of the school. When it comes time to approach the school board, they find themselves alone proclaiming their importance. They suddenly find they should have been advocating for their programs.

When listing the top 10 things you must do this year, is any form of advocacy on your list? Probably not, since advocacy is about building a fan base; and this comes naturally through the delivery of exceptional library service and really doesn't seem to be a part of our job description.

Action Plan? Advocacy? Is that Part of a School Librarian's Job Description?

Although it won't be written out in the job description, advocacy efforts should always be in force, and not simply an eleventh-hour attempt to save a program that is repeatedly and consistently on the chopping block. School library advocacy must be an integral part of the library program.

"It is not enough to care. You must act."[2] School Library Systems—Advocacy Toolkit

If school librarians respond with inaction, then school library services will continue to be underfunded, misunderstood, and diminished. Youngsters will grow up without the opportunity to gain legitimate learning experiences in the library, missing out on information literacy, inquiry learning, quality information resources, and, most importantly, access to books for free, independent reading. If school librarians don't act, then legislators never hear compelling reasons to vote for library standards, library materials funding, and minimum staffing requirements. Speaking up for students and teachers to get the best possible library experience is not the same thing as begging for your own job, but it does mean that school librarians won't stay silent about this very topic in which only they are experts.

Generally, the decision to cut or eliminate library services is recommended by a district's administrators and approved or disapproved by the local school district board of education. The tendency is to blame the cuts on the school board members and proclaim them as the villains, and this may be true in some cases. Usually, though, the state and federal dollars that make up the school budget are simply insufficient to continue programs. The board has to make tough decisions and relies on the district management team to give good advice. Too often, the management team and school board simply don't know what is happening in school libraries. It is up to school librarians to make sure that the management team and the school board members understand that schools revolve around the library program. If tough cuts need to be made, the library is not the place to start. The librarian must be indispensable to the success of teachers and students and support learning every day, and this must be evident to all stakeholders.

Of course, advocacy doesn't start and end with the local school board. Practically every state library association sponsors a legislation day and encourages school librarians to visit the very legislators that set the laws and the budgets that affect school library services. Many school librarians don't feel moved to participate. The underlying assumption is that someone else will do it or do it better. School librarians often feel that they don't know whom to contact, they don't know what to say, and they don't have time to do it. In the end a sense of powerlessness prevails; they feel that their efforts won't make a difference and become resigned to accepting whatever happens.

The funding justifications for cutting school library programs and school library staff should be challenged by showing the direct match between the library's program contribution toward meeting district-wide objectives and goals:

- Raising test scores
- Mentoring and staff development for teachers
- Decreasing student-to-teacher ratios through collaboration
- College readiness

When districts choose to invest in specific areas, show how the library program accomplishes this. One of our strengths as school librarians is adapting more quickly to educational changes than classroom teachers. There has to be a redistribution of the dwindling dollars and new ways of delivering public education. The funding deciders expect pleas for dollars. Change the dynamic by being on their side to problem-solve for the good of the whole. Sue Sheldon:[3]

> The school library has the potential to occupy a central place in the everyday life of teachers and students. The library is the source for most of their recreational reading materials. The school library is also a central meeting place, where groups can gather to discuss both academic topics and their common interests. For many students, it may be their only access to the Internet. If students want to find nonfiction materials written at their reading and interest level, that also supports the topics they are assigned to study, the school library is essentially the only place to go. As such, the library is the hub of the school in a very real way, for information, for socializing, and for entertainment.

Public Libraries Have "Friends of the Library"—School Libraries Must Have Fans!

The school library fan base must be greater than the usual book lovers who frequent libraries everywhere. Reach out to create a wide and varied fan base so that you could fill a school board meeting with persons who will speak up for you and your importance to them.

- Administrators
  The school principal may be the one who recommends reductions should there be a budget shortfall, but if the district imposes reductions, the principal can be

a powerful advocate. Principals can often find funds to save programs they consider important.

District administrators can also be important fans of excellent library programs. They can insist on minimum staffing levels even in the face of budget cuts, which ultimately can make the difference in staff maintaining benefit status.

- Teachers
  Classroom teachers, as a group, can be powerful advocates for the library program. They can speak to how the library program makes them more effective as teachers. They can explain what it means for students to have access and help before, after, and during the school day. They are generally good communicators willing to speak in front of the school board.
- Parents
  Vocal parent support for library programs may be the most powerful deterrent to school boards faced with approving library cuts. Parents are voters, and school boards listen to their constituencies.
- Students
  Many different subgroups of students are on campus for you to cultivate as fans. Usually, you can count on the academically inclined (bookworms, math geeks, or scientists) to speak on your behalf. However, don't forget there are many other groups to cultivate: artists, student council officers, at-risk (potential gang members, stoners, or criminals), athletes, cheerleaders, computer nerds, the emotionally needy, newcomers (English learners and students new to the school), gamers, grade repeaters, musicians (band members, choir members, or rockers), nonconformists (emos, gays, Goths, loners, or wannabes), poor kids, rich kids, skaters, special needs, thespians, tomboys, and any other group to which students self-identify themselves as belonging. If there is a group that needs space to meet or resources that you can provide, you can build that fan base by providing them.

The indispensable school librarian knows that these stakeholders will be willing, ready, and able to stand up and speak out on behalf of the library. This is advocacy at its best.

Notes

1. Rettig, J. "School Libraries and the Educational Ecosystem." *Change: The Magazine of Higher Learning* 41 (2) (2009): 28–29.

2. School Library Systems Association of New York State, http://www.crbsls.org/slsa/.

3. Susan Sheldon, Teacher Librarian Poway Schools, public post on CALIB K12 on April 12, 2009.

CHAPTER 1

Crisis in School Libraries

Practically every day there are news stories about the crisis in education, necessitating reforms and school restructuring. No Child Left Behind (NCLB), Reading First, and an increasing number of intervention plans are meant to support all students in becoming academically proficient or advanced in mathematics and language arts. At the same time, economic difficulties have caused school budgets to shrink, and school librarians are often among the first people cut.

School libraries are targets for these cuts for many reasons:

- Decision-makers don't understand the role of the library in modern schools.
- The library is a cost center that doesn't generate income the way a schoolteacher is linked to average daily attendance (ADA).
- A school library is not always required by the state education code.
- No requirement exists saying that a school library should have a minimum number of open hours.
- No requirement is in place to employ credentialed school librarians, and libraries can be run by clerical staff, volunteers, or the teacher of the visiting class.
- Library and information-literacy standards have not been adopted in all states.
- Library budgets are sometimes set by the whim of the principal, who may have different priorities.

Once library services begin to be cut, a vicious cycle begins. Library services are reduced predicated on the loss of staff/hours. Staff and students do not have access when they need it, generating bad will. Library staffers are demoralized, often working far more hours than paid for or giving up and providing limited service. When further budget cuts are necessary, the library program is seen as expendable.

Increasing cuts to school libraries in many locations and sometimes entire states have led to the current situation in which the tools necessary for learning are missing from many of our schools. Many elementary school libraries are woefully inadequate and are operated largely by library aides and even volunteers, sometimes without a single certified librarian in any capacity to oversee them. Often, severely curtailed hours are available for the students in each building. Collections left unattended tend to migrate from the library to other locations. When no one is focused on the collection, funds to purchase materials dwindle or are spent with little regard to the needs of the school.

Schools and school libraries frequently appear in the news. Here are some headlines found between December 15, 2008, and January 15, 2009.

Headlines

"Ala. gov making biggest education cuts in 48 years"
MSN Money, December 15, 2008

"New twist: Philadelphia branches slated for closing are de facto school libraries"
Library Journal, December 16, 2008

"Empty shelves, filled with imagination"
New York Times, December 19, 2008

"School library budget cuts leave shelves without new books"
Meriden Record-Journal, Connecticut, December 25, 2008

"Newark schools could cut PE, music, library services"
The Newark Advocate, Ohio, January 1, 2009

"Loss of libraries a bad bookend to '08"
New York Daily News, January 5, 2009

"Education budget cuts very likely, lawmakers say"
Lawrence Journal-World, Kansas, January 7, 2009

"Education braces for possible cuts"
Salt Lake Tribune, January 8, 2009

"Governor proposes controversial education cut for California"
MSNBC, January 9, 2009

"Education cuts coming into focus"
News Herald, Florida, January 10, 2009

"Proposed school cuts draw mixed response"
Washington Post, January 11, 2009

Secret Language of Impending Cuts

School librarians may think that their administrators, school board trustees, or legislators simply have no other choice than to cut library programs in abysmal financial times, but this is often not the case. So how can a school librarian tell when decision-makers do not understand and support library programs? Carefully read each of the following statements and see if you can identify the underlying assumptions and justifications.

If they say . . .

"We're keeping the cuts away from the classroom, so we have to sacrifice physical education, art and music programs, and library service."

The library is immediately dismissed as being a "classroom," although it is generally the biggest classroom in the school that serves the entire student body and faculty.

"With computers and the Internet becoming ubiquitous, the role libraries will play in the schools of the future is uncertain."

This clearly shows a misunderstanding of the multiple functions of the school library. Additionally, there is no evidence that library attendance and usage has decreased due to the Internet.

"We are working to have the cuts directly affect the students as little as possible—by cutting non-essential services like libraries, art, music, and physical education."

Again, this reduces the importance of the library from something you must have to something that is "nice" to have.

"Too many students can't read at a basic level. What is the point of having a library open when the kids can't read the books? The library program needs to be temporarily downsized so that the money spent there can be diverted to hiring intervention reading teachers. The library program will be reinstated when all the students are reading at grade level."

This is exactly the opposite of what makes sense if you read the research on reading skills for children. If students are having trouble reading, then access to a wide variety of books for pleasure reading is exactly what many of them need.[1] Ironically, these programs take away all choice of reading matter and subject students to tedious phonics books, fluency cards, and excessive "high interest-low level" nonfiction passages with requisite comprehension questions.

"Everything is on the table. Library staff, class-size reduction, athletics, transportation, and custodial services are all potentially facing spending cuts."

This is meant to assuage everyone's feelings that they are being picked on, that the pain will be equally shared, and that there will be a fair process to decide the areas that will be cut. Notice that administrator positions are rarely mentioned as something that is "on the table."

"We've already cut libraries, support staff, and school nurses. There really is no fat left."

This statement implies that libraries are the "fat"—and that teachers and students don't care about or need library services. This shows they do not understand that the library adds value to the academic program, and says instead that only classroom teachers are important for student success. It basically implies that libraries don't matter.

Advocacy Efforts and Toolkits

Another indicator of the crisis in school libraries is the number of advocacy campaigns and toolkits that are being made available to help school librarians and their supporters in saving their programs. You may be able to adapt information from them to help build your advocacy program.

American Association of School Libraries (AASL)
http://www.ala.org/ala/mgrps/divs/aasl/aaslissues/toolkits/aasladvocacy.cfm
Resources are here to be used by any school library. The kit includes a strategic marketing plan for school library media centers, including a PowerPoint presentation that can be downloaded and customized. The toolkit provides key talking points, sample letters to the editor, and a variety of research studies, white papers, and links to additional resources. A downloadable file introduces advocacy and provides training for spreading the message. Additionally, there is a nationwide campaign to raise awareness of school libraries and their importance linked to the ALA's successful @ Your Library campaign.

California School Library Association
http://www.csla.net/
There is detailed information here along with an interactive toolkit to respond to a March 15 notice.

Colorado Library Consortium
http://www.clicweb.org/library_community/advocacy.php
This is a remarkable clearinghouse that is well organized to help you navigate the many different resources available from other organizations.

Friends of Santa Cruz School Libraries
http://foslsantacruz.org/
You'll find videos about school libraries and more than 30 helpful links.

LMC Source
http://www.lmcsource.com/tech/power/2nd/power2.htm
School library programs make a difference. This is the accompanying Web site to the book of the same name by Dr. David Loertscher and Keith Curry Lance. Included here are 12 short PowerPoint presentations that help address topics of concern when library programs are threatened.

Minnesota Educational Media Organization
http://www.memoweb.org/
This organization has a special link called "When Your Job Is on the Line." It lists eight strategies that can be implemented immediately.

A video is included that can be played to highlight the importance of school library programs with accompanying handouts to be given to principals and parents.

North Carolina School Library Media Association
http://www.ncslma.org/Advocacy.htm
Included here are sample "elevator speeches," short answers to important questions that can be delivered in the space of an elevator ride. Their marketing plan can be downloaded as a PDF.

School Library Systems Association of New York State Advocacy Toolkit
http://www.crbsls.org/slsa/
The sunflower action plan has key talking points, contacts, sample letters, testimony for stakeholder groups, and advocacy links to additional resources. They provide a consistent look and feel to their advocacy by using sunflowers and bright yellow paper on all their communication.

Pennsylvania School Librarians Association
http://www.psla.org/pslaworkshops/pslaworkshops.php4
This organization presents advocacy workshops, and the accompanying handouts, presentation notes, and tools are posted online for everyone to use.

While there is no shortage of advice on ways to save library programs, they all depend on one thing. The library programs must be exceptional, and the school librarians involved in programs under fire must be willing to go above and beyond the call of duty. Mediocre programs and lukewarm school librarians and their staff will not survive. Additionally, waiting until library programs are threatened to begin advocacy will likely mean that it is too late. Building support for libraries must be a regular part of a school librarian's job.

Note

1. To read more about the importance of free voluntary reading in the development of literacy, consult Stephen Krashen's Web site, http://www.sdkrashen.com/.

CHAPTER 2

State Guidelines for School Libraries in the United States

When the U.S. Constitution was written, it was agreed that states would retain the rights to govern all issues not covered by the Constitution. This means that education of the citizens of each state is under the authority of that state. In most states, this authority is given to a department of education, and the person responsible for this role may be elected or appointed. Either way, the person in charge holds a very political position.

Most states also have a board made up of persons to help oversee the department of education. This board will determine what is required of a student to graduate, and it may even mandate subjects to be taught. Physical education classes can be required and even a particular test of physical strength may be in place. State boards usually mandate the teaching of that state's history and often the grade level at which this will be taught. Much of this can be found in the state's education code.

A state's education code may or may not mandate library service in spite of the research that shows the impact of school libraries on student achievement. "Even before NCLB, studies in Colorado, Pennsylvania, and Iowa demonstrated that professional school librarians and school libraries make irreplaceable contributions to student achievement ("School Libraries Work!," 2008).[1]

These replicated studies show that schools with libraries operated by a state-certified school librarian report better learning outcomes and meet state-established NCLB achievement criteria at significantly higher rates than schools lacking this basic service. The following list gives details for each state in the United States. All resource links were working as of January 23, 2010, but are subject to change.

♥ Look for the states that have a mandate regarding school library services.[2]
🖥 Web site address for more information, generally through the state department of education.

● Certification/credential requirements for teacher-librarians.

▤ Standards: Some are for students to master and some are for school librarians to implement.

⁂ Associations.

👫 Student-to-media-specialist ratio.

ALABAMA

Alabama Department of Education

⌨ http://www.alsde.edu

● Master's degree and teacher certificate required

▤ Information Literacy Standards, http://alex.state.al.us/browseallStand. php

⁂ Alabama Instructional Media Association, http://www.alaima.org

👫 437:1

ALASKA

Alaska Department of Education & Early Development

⌨ http://www.eed.state.ak.us

● School librarians are issued a Type C certificate

▤ Library/Information Literacy Standards, http://www.eed.state.ak.us/standards/pdf/standards.pdf

⁂ Alaska Association of School Libraries (part of Alaska Library Association), http://www.akla.org/akasl/

👫 1,268:1

ARIZONA

Arizona Department of Education

⌨ http://www.ade.az.gov

● Teacher's certificate and one year of teaching experience required, http://www.ade.az.gov/certification/requirements/Endorsements/LibraryMedia.pdf

▤ Research and Information Literacy (found in Strand 3, Educational Technology Standards),
http://www.ade.az.gov/standards/technology/Articulated_Grade_Level/

⁂ Arizona Library Association (there is a teacher-librarian section), http://www.azla.org

👫 1,009:1

ARKANSAS

♥ *Full-time media specialist mandated for all schools with more than 300 students.*

Arkansas Department of Education

⌨ http://arkansased.org/

● Master's degree and teacher certificate required

▤ Library/Media Framework, http://www.arkansased.org/teachers/frameworks2.html#library

✵ Arkansas Association of Instructional Media, http://aaim.k12.ar.us/

✵ Arkansas Association of School Librarians (part of Arkansas Library Association), http://www.arlib.org/AASL/index.htm

⚏ 437:1

CALIFORNIA

California Department of Education

⌨ http://www.cde.ca.gov

⚘ Teacher-librarian certification, http://www.ctc.ca.gov/credentials/CREDS/library-media.html

▤ Library standards are in the process of being written

✵ California School Library Association, http://www.csla.net/

⚏ 4,363:1

COLORADO

Colorado Department of Education

⌨ http://www.cde.state.co.us

⚘ Master's degree and teacher certificate required, http://www.cde.state.co.us/cdeprof/Licensure_addendorsment_info.asp

▤ National Information Literacy Standards (ALA) are referenced, http://www.cde.state.co.us/litstandards/litstandards.htm

✵ Colorado Association of School Librarians (a subdivision of Colorado Association of Libraries), http://www.cal-webs.org/

⚏ 800:1

CONNECTICUT

Connecticut State Department of Education

⌨ http://www.sde.ct.gov/sde/site/default.asp

⚘ Must be eligible for certification as a classroom teacher, http://www.sde.ct.gov/sde/cwp/view.asp?a=2613&Q=321230

▤ Information and Technology Literacy Framework, http://www.sde.ct.gov/sde/lib/sde/pdf/Curriculum/itf.pdf

✵ Connecticut Association of School Librarians, http://www.ctcasl.com/

⚏ 955:1

DELAWARE

Delaware Department of Education

⌨ http://www.doe.k12.de.us

⚘ Master's degree required, http://deeds.doe.k12.de.us/default.aspx

▤ Research & Information Literacy are referenced in English Language Arts and Social Studies, http://www.doe.k12.de.us/infosuites/staff/ci/content_areas/ela.shtml

✵ Delaware School Library Media Association, http://www.udel.edu/erc/dslma/

⚏ 1,052:1

FLORIDA
Florida Department of Education
💻 http://www.fldoe.org
🍎 Educational media specialist (does not require teaching certificate), http://www.fldoe.org/edcert/rules/6A-4-0251.asp
📄 Information literacy, http://www.fldoe.org/educators/standards.as
👥 Florida Association for Media in Education, http://www.floridamedia.org/
👪 869:1

GEORGIA
♥ *Full-time media specialist is mandated in all schools exceeding 251 students.*
Georgia Department of Education
💻 http://www.doe.k12.ga.us/
🍎 Media specialist certificate, http://www.gapsc.com
📄 None specific to libraries, http://www.gadoe.org/ci_services.aspx
👥 Georgia Library Media Association, http://glma-inc.org/
👪 733:1

HAWAII
♥ *Full-time media specialist is mandated in all schools.*
Hawaii Department of Education
💻 http://doe.k12.hi.us
🍎 School librarian—master's degree required, http://www.htsb.org/html/details/teacherstandards/librarians.html
📄 None specific to libraries, http://doe.k12.hi.us/curriculum/
👥 Hawaii Association of School Librarians, http://hasl.ws/
👪 670:1

IDAHO
Idaho State Department of Education
💻 http://www.sde.idaho.gov/
🍎 Teacher's certificate required—special endorsement for education media generalist, http://www.sde.idaho.gov/site/teacher_certification/subject_area.htm#25
📄 None specific to libraries, http://www.sde.idaho.gov/site/content_standards/
👥 Idaho Library Association, http://www.idaholibraries.org/
👪 1,310:1

ILLINOIS
Illinois State Board of Education
💻 http://www.isbe.state.il.us/
🍎 http://www.isbe.state.il.us/certification/default.htm
📄 None specific to libraries, http://www.isbe.net/ils/
👥 Illinois School Library Media Association, http://www.islma.org/
👪 1,052:1

INDIANA

Indiana Department of Education

🖥 http://www.doe.state.in.us/

🍎 Teacher's certificate required—teacher of library and media, http://www. doe.in.gov/educatorlicensing/LibraryMediaContStds.html

📄 None specific to libraries, http://dc.doe.in.gov/Standards/Academic Standards/StandardSearch.aspx

⁜ Indiana Library Federation, http://www.ilfonline.org/

👪 1,006:1

IOWA

Iowa Department of Education

🖥 http://www.iowa.gov/educate/

🍎 Master's degree required

📄 None specific to libraries, http://www.iowa.gov/educate

⁜ Iowa Association of School Libraries, http://www.iasl-ia.org/

👪 659:1

KANSAS

Kansas State Department of Education

🖥 http://www.ksde.org/

🍎 Master's degree and teacher's certificate required

📄 Library Media & Technology Model Standards, http://www.ksde.org/ Default.aspx?tabid=3511#lmtStd

⁜ Kansas Association of School Libraries, http://kasl.typepad.com/

👪 458:1

KENTUCKY

Kentucky Department of Education

🖥 http://education.ky.gov/KDE/

🍎 Teacher's certificate required

📄 None directly related to libraries

⁜ Kentucky School Media Association, http://www.kysma.org/

👪 521:1

LOUISIANA

Louisiana Department of Education

🖥 http://www.doe.state.la.us

🍎 None mandated

📄 Educational Technology Standards, http://www.doe.state.la.us/lde/saa/ 1222.html

⁜ Louisiana Library Association, http://www.llaonline.org/

👪 680:1

MAINE
Maine Department of Education
- 🖥 http://www.maine.gov/education/index.shtml
- ♥ None mandated
- 📄 None directly related to libraries
- ⚹ Maine Association of School Libraries, http://www.maslibraries.org/
- 👪 733:1

MARYLAND
♥ *Full-time media specialist is mandated in all schools with more than 200 students.*
Maryland State Department of Education
- 🖥 http://www.marylandpublicschools.org/MSDE
- ♥ Master's degree required
- 📄 Standards for school library media programs in Maryland (within technology plan), http://www.marylandpublicschools.org
- ⚹ Maryland Association of School Librarians, http://www.maslmd.org/
- 👪 863:1

MASSACHUSETTS
Massachusetts Department of Education
- 🖥 http://www.doe.mass.edu
- ♥ Teacher's certificate required
- 📄 None directly related to libraries
- ⚹ Massachusetts School Library Association, http://www.maschoolibraries.org/
- 👪 1,498:1

MICHIGAN
Michigan Department of Education
- 🖥 http://www.michigan.gov/mde
- ♥ Teacher's certificate required
- 📄 None directly related to libraries
- ⚹ Michigan Association for Media in Education, http://www.mimame.org/
- 👪 1,052:1

MINNESOTA
Minnesota Department of Education
- 🖥 http://education.state.mn.us/mde/index.html
- ♥ None mandated
- 📄 None directly related to libraries
- ⚹ Minnesota Educational Media Organization, http://memotech.ning.com/
- 👪 833:1

MISSISSIPPI
♥ *Full-time media specialist is mandated in all schools with more than 500 students.*
Mississippi Department of Education
🖳 http://www.mde.k12.ms.us/
🛡 None mandated
📄 None directly related to libraries
✣ Mississippi Library Association, http://www.misslib.org/index.php/organization/sections/school-library/
👥 689:1

MISSOURI
♥ *Full-time media specialist is mandated in all schools with more than 800 students.*
Missouri Department of Elementary and Secondary Education
🖳 http://dese.mo.gov/
🛡 Teacher's certificate required
📄 None directly related to libraries
✣ Missouri Association of School Librarians, http://www.maslonline.org/
👥 559:1

MONTANA
♥ *Full-time media specialist is mandated in all schools with more than 251 students.*
Montana Office of Public Instruction
🖳 http://www.opi.mt.gov/
🛡 None mandated
📄 Information Literacy/Library Media Standards have been replaced by Common Core Standards, http://www.opi.mt.gov/Curriculum
✣ Montana Library Association, http://www.mtlib.org/
👥 466:1

NEBRASKA
♥ *Full-time media specialist is mandated in all schools with more than 750 students.*
Nebraska Department of Education
🖳 http://www.nde.state.ne.us/
🛡 Teacher's certificate required
📄 Multiple Literacies, http://www.nde.state.ne.us/Assessment/Standards.htm
✣ Nebraska Educational Media Association, http://www.schoollibrariesrock.org/
👥 511:1

NEVADA
Nevada Department of Education
🖳 http://www.doe.nv.gov/
🛡 Teacher's certificate required
📄 Information Literacy Standards, http://www.anystandard.net/teachNV.jpg

⁂ Nevada Library Association, http://www.nevadalibraries.org/index.html
⁂ Clark County School Library Association, http://www.ccsd.net/libassoc/index.html
👪 1,157:1

NEW HAMPSHIRE
New Hampshire Department of Education
💻 http://www.ed.state.nh.us/education/
🛡 None mandated
📄 None directly related to libraries
⁂ New Hampshire Educational Media Association, http://www.nhema.net/
👪 701:1

NEW JERSEY
New Jersey Department of Education
💻 http://www.nj.gov/education/
🛡 Master's degree required
📄 2009 Standards Revision Project, http://www.state.nj.us/education/cccs/2009/final.htm
⁂ New Jersey Association of School Librarians, http://www.njasl.org/
👪 672:1

NEW MEXICO
New Mexico Public Education Department
💻 http://www.ped.state.nm.us/
🛡 Teacher's certificate required
📄 None directly related to libraries
⁂ New Mexico Library Association, http://nmla.org/
👪 1,220:1

NEW YORK
🛡 *Full-time media specialist is mandated in all middle and high schools.*
New York State Education Department
💻 http://www.nysed.gov/
🛡 Master's degree required
📄 None directly related to libraries
⁂ Long Island School Media Association, http://bobrowen.com/lisma/
New York Library Association—School Library Media Section, http://www.nyla.org/index.php?page_id=52
👪 860:1

NORTH CAROLINA
North Carolina Department of Public Instruction
💻 http://www.dpi.state.nc.us/organization/
🛡 Master's degree required
📄 Information Skills, http://www.ncpublicschools.org/curriculum/

⁂ North Carolina School Library Media Association, http://www.ncslma.org/

👬 569:1

NORTH DAKOTA

North Dakota Department of Public Instruction

💻 http://www.dpi.state.nd.us/

🛡 Teacher's certificate required

📄 Yes, Library/Technology Literacy, http://www.dpi.state.nd.us/standard/content.shtm

⁂ North Dakota Library Association: School Library and Youth Section, http://www.ndla.info/

⁂ North Dakota Education Association: Library Media Association Section, http://www.ndea.org/

👬 312:1

OHIO

Ohio Department of Education

💻 http://www.ode.state.oh.us/GD/Templates/Pages/ODE/ODEDefault-Page. aspx?page=1

🛡 Library/media license required

📄 Yes, Guidelines for Effective School Library Media Programs (not students)

📄 Technology Standards—Technology and Information Literacy Strand, http://www.genevaschools.org/standards/#technology

⁂ Ohio Educational Library Media Association, http://www.oelma.org/

👬 1,107:1

OKLAHOMA

♥ *Full-time media specialist is mandated in all schools with more than 500 students.*

Oklahoma State Department of Education

💻 http://sde.state.ok.us/

🛡 None mandated

📄 None related directly to libraries

⁂ Oklahoma Association of School Library Media Specialists

👬 636:1

OREGON

♥ *One full-time media specialist is mandated per district.*

Oregon Department of Education

💻 http://www.ode.state.or.us/

🛡 Teacher's certificate required

📄 Educational Technology Standards, http://www.ode.state.or.us/search/page/?id=1880

⁂ Oregon Association of School Libraries, http://www.oema.net/

👬 451:1

PENNSYLVANIA
Pennsylvania Department of Education
💻 http://www.pde.state.pa.us/
♥ Teaching certificate with endorsement in school librarianship
📄 None specific to libraries
✳ Pennsylvania Library Association, http://www.psla.org/
👪 825:1

RHODE ISLAND
♥ *Full-time media specialist is mandated in all high schools.*
Rhode Island Department of Elementary and Secondary Education
💻 http://www.ride.ri.gov/
♥ None mandated
📄 School Library and Information Literacy Framework, http://www.ri.net/
RIEMA/infolit.html
✳ Rhode Island Educational Media Association, http://riedmedia.org/
👪 522:1

SOUTH CAROLINA
♥ *Full-time media specialist is mandated in high schools and middle schools with more than 400 students and elementary schools with more than 375 students.*
South Carolina Department of Education
💻 http://ed.sc.gov/
♥ Master's degree required
📄 None specific to libraries
✳ South Carolina Association of School Librarians, http://www.scasl.net/
👪 576:1

SOUTH DAKOTA
South Dakota Department of Education
💻 http://ed.sc.gov/
♥ None mandated
📄 South Dakota School Library Standards, http://doe.sd.gov/content
standards/
✳ South Dakota Library Association, http://www.sdlibraryassociation.org/
👪 658:1

TENNESSEE
♥ *Full-time media specialist is mandated in K–8 schools with more than 550 students and high schools with more than 300 students.*
Tennessee Education
💻 http://www.state.tn.us/education/
♥ Master's degree required
📄 None specific to libraries
✳ Tennessee Association of School Librarians, http://www.discoveret.org/tasl/
👪 645:1

TEXAS
Texas Education Agency
- 🖳 http://www.tea.state.tx.us/index.aspx
- ♥ Master's degree required
- 📄 School Library Programs: Guidelines and Standards (not for students), http://www.tsl.state.tx.us/ld/schoollibs/
- ⚛ Texas Library Association/Texas Association of School Librarians, http://www.discoveret.org/tasl/
- 🏃 773:1

UTAH
Utah State Office of Education
- 🖳 http://www.usoe.k12.ut.us/
- ♥ Teacher's certificate required
- 📄 Library Media Standards (includes both student standards and program standards), http://www.uen.org/core/
- ⚛ Utah Library Association, http://www.ula.org/
- 🏃 1,650:1

VERMONT
- ♥ *Full-time media specialist is mandated in all schools with more than 300 students.*
Vermont Department of Education
- 🖳 http://www.education.vermont.gov/
- ♥ Teacher's certification required
- 📄 Information Technology Standards are written, but libraries are not tasked with teaching the content, http://education.vermont.gov/new/html/pubs/framework.html
- ⚛ Vermont School Library Association, http://vsla.info/
- 🏃 455:1

VIRGINIA
- ♥ *Full-time media specialist is mandated in all schools with more than 300 students.*
Virginia Department of Education
- 🖳 http://www.doe.virginia.gov/
- ♥ None mandated
- 📄 Research is a portion of the Computer Technology Standards, http://www.doe.virginia.gov/testing/sol/standards_docs/index.shtml
- ⚛ Virginia Library Association—School Library Section, http://www.vla.org/demo/School-Lib/Index.html
- 🏃 782:1

WASHINGTON
Washington Office of Superintendent of Public Instruction
- 🖳 http://www.k12.wa.us/
- ♥ Teacher's certificate required

📄 None directly related to libraries

⚹ Washington Library Media Association, http://www.wlma.org/

👫 741:1

WEST VIRGINIA

West Virgina Department of Education

💻 http://wvde.state.wv.us/

♥ None mandated

📄 Twenty-first-century learning skills are listed and information literacy is one component, but the library is not mentioned, http://wvde.state.wv.us/policies/csos.html

⚹ West Virginia Library Association—School Library Division, http://www.wvla.org/index.html

👫 852:1

WISCONSIN

♥ *Full-time media specialist is mandated in all high schools, middle schools, and elementary schools and must be supervised by a library media specialist.*

Wisconsin Department of Public Instruction

💻 http://dpi.wi.gov/

♥ Teacher's certificate required

📄 Information and Technology Literacy, http://dpi.wi.gov/standards/

⚹ Wisconsin Library Association, http://www.wla.lib.wi.us/membership/

👫 661:1

WYOMING

Wyoming Department of Education

💻 http://www.k12.wy.us

♥ None mandated

📄 None directly related to libraries

⚹ Wyoming Library Association—School Library Section, http://www.wyla.org/schools/

👫 772:1

This list will be very helpful to you if your state is one that has no mention of school libraries in its code. You can look for a state that is similar in population size and see if they have something in place that makes your situation look bad. Using the "keep up with the Joneses" is sometimes a good approach when talking with state boards of education. They can be powerful allies if you state your case well because they have the power to make some decisions and then carry them to the state legislature.

School librarians need to visit their state legislators frequently to keep them informed of the role of the school librarian and the impact a good school library can make with student achievement. Going just to report what's going on in your area helps you establish a rapport with this person and the office staff. You may not see the legislator each time you go, but you can meet with the staff person. It is also helpful if you can take along a parent, a teacher, and some students to help you make your report.

Establishing your situation with this office means they know who you are and what you do. Then, when you ask for support for a piece of legislation, it will be much easier than only going into that office when you are going to ask for something.

Mandating school library programs and encouraging funding for school libraries is not an easy task. It will take the support of all school librarians working with their professional associations, and hopefully with the endorsement of their teachers and administrators to make changes. It is not a one-shot deal. It takes repeated efforts over time, and a well-planned, well-executed effort to make these things happen and to halt any erosion once progress is in place.

Notes

1. "School Libraries Work!" (2008), from http://www2.scholastic.com/content/collateral_resources/pdf/s/slw3_2008.pdf. Accessed October 15, 2009.

2. Everhart, N. "Filling the Void." *School Library Journal* (June 1, 2002), from http://www.schoollibraryjournal.com/index.asp?layout=article&articleid=CA219977. Accessed November 25, 2009.

CHAPTER 3

The AttrACTive Librarian

Getting the students and teachers to come to the library is the first step to making yourself essential on campus. This chapter begins with a list of attrACTion items for you to implement, defines *attraction* as we are using it in terms of school librarians, and provides you with a quiz to see how well you score. Analysis of your scores and a series of questions and answers will help you become an attrACTive librarian.

Ten "AttrACTion" Action Items for Every School Librarian

Do:

✓ Present yourself as a competent, essential member of the faculty
✓ Create an attractive space
✓ Host meaningful programs
✓ Provide exceptional service to your patrons
✓ Attract patrons to your library
✓ Broadcast what is happening inside your library
✓ Reduce barriers to access
✓ Evaluate yourself and your library program
✓ Use the results of the evaluation to create realistic goals that support strategic improvements
✓ Challenge decision-makers to reexamine their image of you and your library—change the old stereotype to reflect a twenty-first-century learning commons

Our definitions:
attract

1. Direct toward the school library by means of some psychological power or physical attributes. *The school library attracts students, teachers, and parents.*

2. To arouse interest or desire in visiting the school library. *I was attracted to the library when the librarian strode past wearing a Cinderella-style gown and a tiara . . . what was going on?*

attraction

1. The force by which the school librarian entices a person to enter. *The student couldn't resist the attraction of the window display and entered the library to find out more.*
2. An entertainment that the school librarian offers to the patrons. *Don't miss the best attraction at the open house—the open-mike poetry reading in the school library.*
3. The school library as a place, sponsor of an event, or pleasant area that patrons want to visit. *The library is consistently listed as one of the top five attractions on the school campus.*

attractive

1. Pleasing to the eye or mind especially through beauty or charm. *It is a remarkably attractive library with comfortable seating and plenty of space to work.*
2. Enticing to patrons and eliciting engagement. *Nothing is as attractive as a warm library on a chilly winter morning.*

Attraction Quiz

1. My library media center staff is professionally dressed and groomed.
   Criteria: cleanliness, makeup, jewelry, fragrance, hair, and attire. If your principal or superintendent walked in, would you hide yourself or others behind the circulation desk in hopes that your jeans and flip-flops wouldn't be seen? Is there a sexual harassment case ready to be filed?

   Interview ready 10 – 9 – 8 – 7 – 6 – Adequate 5 – 4 – 3 – 2 – 1 Super casual – Problem area

2. My library media center is represented at faculty meetings and on important school committees.
   Criteria: Are you kept "in the know" about what is happening elsewhere on campus? Is the library seen as a resource for curriculum and what is happening in the classrooms (for example; professional learning communities, response to intervention assessment, etc.)? Someone from the library is serving as a member of at least some of the important groups on campus; PTA, School Site Council, Technology Committee, etc.

   Well connected 10 – 9 – 8 – 7 – 6 – Somewhat informed 5 – 4 – 3 – 2 – 1 No clue

3. My library media center provides an inviting environment.
   Criteria: Colorful, welcoming, artwork displayed, child-friendly for elementaries, engaging sophistication for middle and high schools, perhaps whimsical or creative. Ultimately, you can measure this by the crowd level you usually maintain. Is it a whirlwind or practically empty?

   Fascinating 10 – 9 – 8 – 7 – 6 – Average 5 – 4 – 3 – 2 – 1 Boring

4. My library media center is conducive to student learning.
   Criteria: Students often come to the library to do meaningful work or study. The librarian maintains a climate that is quiet enough that it doesn't disturb students trying to read or study, but not so restrictive that group work cannot be done.

   Thriving 10 – 9 – 8 – 7 – 6 – Average 5 – 4 – 3 – 2 – 1 Stagnant

5. My library media center allows full access for all students.
   Criteria: Students can come to the library as needed during the entire instructional day, and additionally before and after school. The library is not closed during the librarian's lunch or break periods. Students can visit even if another class is scheduled.

   Fully open 10 – 9 – 8 – 7 – 6 – Partially open 5 – 4 – 3 – 2 – 1 Often closed or limited access

6. The arrangement of my library media center permits visual control of the entire center from the circulation and/or office area.
   Criteria: Are there any "blind spots" where students can be hidden from the librarian's sight?

   Completely viewable 10 – 9 – 8 – 7 – 6 – Some blind spots 5 – 4 – 3 – 2 – 1 Lots of nooks and crannies

7. My library media center has seating for large groups, small groups, and individual study.
   Criteria: Are there enough tables, carrels, and reading areas? Are there comfortable places to read? If this is an elementary school, is there a story area with enough floor space to allow even the largest class to sit on the floor comfortably.

   Spacious and well accommodated 10 – 9 – 8 – 7 – 6 – Serviceable 5 – 4 – 3 – 2 – 1 Inadequate

8. My library media center has shelving and seating that is appropriately sized and constructed for my school's population.
   Criteria: Is there a danger that your shelving could collapse, fall apart, or tip over? Do the shelves look completely packed, or is there enough area to display books with the cover out? If you have primary students, can they reach the shelves they need without using a step stool? Do students look comfortable when seated? Do their legs dangle in too-tall chairs or are they sitting in chairs too small for them?

   Model Quality 10 – 9 – 8 – 7 – 6 – Adequate 5 – 4 – 3 – 2 – 1 Inadequate

9. My library media center has proper lighting for designated areas and tasks.
   Criteria: Is there natural light coming in from windows or skylights? If the ceiling lighting is inadequate, have floor lamps or table lamps been added? Is there lighting within the furniture or stacks to help patrons?

   Illuminated 10 – 9 – 8 – 7 – 6 – Adequate 5 – 4 – 3 – 2 – 1 Cavelike

10. My library media center has sufficient computers and the electrical and networking outlets to accommodate technology.
    Criteria: Do you have many times during the day when the wait to use the computers discourages students from using the library or only during peak periods like lunch? Can you plug every device directly into a socket or do you need multiple surge protectors with six or eight additional plug spots? Do you have one surge protector plugged into another? Are there wires running everywhere in plain view? Do you have wires taped down onto the carpet or covered with rugs or wire covers so that no one will trip on them?

    Wired and ready 10 – 9 – 8 – 7 – 6 – Adequate 5 – 4 – 3 – 2 – 1 Shockingly inadequate

11. My library media center has a well-placed circulation desk and other furniture meant for use in a library, and was chosen to support library tasks.
Criteria: Is the circulation desk close to the entrance and/or exit and easily accessible? Is there a book drop? Can students easily leave without properly checking out their materials? Is there staff seating that is comfortable during circulation, or do they have to stand or perch on a high stool? Can students reach the counter?

Model Quality 10 – 9 – 8 – 7 – 6 – Adequate 5 – 4 – 3 – 2 – 1 Hodgepodge of castoffs

12. My library media has professional looking, adequately sized signage to facilitate location and use of materials and services.
Criteria: Can students locate most sections without asking for help, i.e., fiction, reference, picture books, and nonfiction? Within nonfiction, are there numbers AND text describing most major areas (folktales, poetry, biography, etc.). Are the signs attractive and up-to-date or has the collection shifted and are the signs out of synch? Are pictures included to help nonreaders?

Super signs 10 – 9 – 8 – 7 – 6 – Adequate 5 – 4 – 3 – 2 – 1 What signs?

13. My library media center is aesthetically pleasing.
Criteria: The arrangement of furniture, stacks, study areas, computer centers, and story areas makes visual sense and doesn't seem cramped or contrived. There are decorative items that enhance the library, such as plants, posters, puppets, stuffed animals related to literature, etc. The building itself is in good repair, without ceiling leaks, cracks, peeling paint, or other structural problems. The library is soundproofed so that you don't have to compete with plumbing noises, loud cafeterias, multipurpose rooms, or classrooms.

Picture ready 10 – 9 – 8 – 7 – 6 – Adequate 5 – 4 – 3 – 2 – 1 Lucky not to be condemned

14. My library media center has sufficient dedicated storage and workspace in close range.
Criteria: Where are new items entered and processed? Is it at the main circulation desk? If you have a lot of new items, where can you store them? Are there stacks of boxes in plain sight or tucked away under tables? If you are in charge of textbooks or teacher materials, are you expected to store them across campus in a shed or bookroom?

Space to spare 10 – 9 – 8 – 7 – 6 – Adequate 5 – 4 – 3 – 2 – 1 Crammed or scattered

15. My library media center communicates evidence of the library's program and activities outside of the library.
Criteria: Are there one or more bulletin boards around campus that the library can use to promote events, and are these current and changed frequently? Are library events featured on the marquee? Is there a library newsletter, or does the school newsletter have a regular space to showcase library events? Is there a library Web site that is kept current and accurate, or is it a static site that never changes?

PR savvy 10 – 9 – 8 – 7 – 6 – Some evidence 5 – 4 – 3 – 2 – 1 Unless you open the door, you'd never even know we have a library

Scoring: Add up your scores.
150–140 Practically a perfect school library (you probably don't need this book)

139–120 Lots of nice features
119–100 Adequate, but nothing special
99–60 There's plenty of room for improvement
59–30 This library is in crisis
29–0 Might as well bomb it

Setting Realistic Objectives

Use the results of the quiz to set objectives for your library. If you have a very low score, it is probably unrealistic to think that you can improve to a very high score in a short time. Making a strategic list of achievable objectives and presenting this to those who can help you make them happen is the first step to improvement.

Look at your responses that have scores of 3, 2, or 1. These scores indicate that this is an area where your library is in crisis. These should become your immediate objectives. Decide if this is an area you can control and change or not. For example, you can change the way you are dressed and groomed. You can add floor and table lamps to adjust or improve lighting. You can probably change the way the library is arranged and decorated. As far as signage goes, you can create signs that look decent with just a word-processing program. However, there are features that aren't easy to change, especially without specialized help or money, such as inadequate wiring, the location of the library, and the number of hours you are paid to work. If you cannot make the changes alone, you can approach decision-makers and groups such as the PTA to "plant the seeds" that these are areas that need improvement. See if you can move these scores to at least 4 within a 12-month period.

For scores of 4, 5, or 6, you might write long-term goals. Just having an adequate or moderately inadequate library is not going to inspire much loyalty or support. However, since none of these features are actually indicating a crisis, you will have to work harder to generate interest in finding help to make your library better. Again, you must separate what you can change on your own and what you cannot. Write goals to communicate and write them in a positive form. For example, if you scored between 4 and 6 for *My library media center has sufficient computers, and the electrical and networking outlets to accommodate technology*, you then need to look at ways to improve that score. Look at each part of the problem and write a goal that addresses it. Then approach the people or groups that might help you and ask them to support your goal.

Problem 1
Not enough computers

Measurable objective
To increase the number of computers for students to use by 50 percent (from 10 to 15)

Who can help?

- Principal
- School site council
- PTA
- Technology committee
- Local business partner
- Grants

Problem 2
Wiring is a mess; wires are loose, tangled, and unsightly.

Measurable objective
To increase the safety of students and staff by preventing and reducing accidents and incidents by organizing, covering, or tying down wires (from four incidents in 2009).

Who can help?

- Safety committee
- Custodian
- Maintenance department
- Information systems or information technology department

Problem 3
Power outlets and network ports are in poor areas or are inadequate for the number of devices being used.

Measurable objective
To modernize the library infrastructure to accommodate twenty-first-century learning by installing a power pole in the area where the 12 student computers are located.

Who can help?

- Bond committee
- Building or maintenance department
- Custodian

Note that in problem 3 it would be unrealistic to expect the changes to be quick or inexpensive. Additionally, whenever building modifications or maintenance is involved, it may be disruptive to library services.

Finally, look at your scores of 7 and higher. These are your strengths that you need to advertise. Although you can incorporate these areas into goals to improve and fine-tune your excellence, you can word these goals somewhat differently. For example:

- Continue to develop the library Web site to make it easier for students to use.

- Evaluate signage on a regular basis to make sure that collection shifts don't create inaccuracies.
- Purchase a new story rug because the old one is faded and worn.

Another smart move is to find out how your library is NOT meeting the needs of your user groups. It is hard to hear it, but asking others for constructive criticism or feedback is critical to making sure that you are meeting the needs of your patrons.

Example: *"If one thing about our school's library media center could be changed, what should it be?"*

This may generate fantastic visions, like reading lofts, creative comfortable seating, or computer lounges, but most likely you will find out that there are areas in even the most exemplary school library that can be improved.

Challenging the Stereotype

The perception of librarians as middle-aged spinsters with hair buns persists despite significant evidence to the contrary. Additionally, principals and teachers may have not had good experiences with school librarians as children or in their professional lives. These experiences often contribute to the perpetuation of the librarian stereotype.

Q & A

Q: What does the stereotyping of librarians have to do with my school library and me?

A: S. I. Hayakawa, the authority on semantics, has written: "The danger of stereotypes lies not in their existence, but in the fact that they become for all people some of the time, and for some people all the time, substitutes for observation."[1] Stereotypes are fixed impressions that are often exaggerations of real characteristics, and they influence our thoughts and actions. While many stereotypes are based solely on physical appearance, the image of librarians may also be influenced by past interactions. The danger of stereotyping librarians (and library services) is that it simplifies the role and function of the school library to a narrow role that doesn't represent what exists at all or even most libraries today. These stereotypes are obstacles for most school librarians because decision-makers and potential patrons will not take the time to find out the real scope of services and might make judgments based on these inaccurate simplifications.

As far as the librarian stereotype, the media is in large part responsible. In 1984, for an episode of the *Family Feud* game show, a group of 100 people were surveyed and asked what they believed to be typical "librarian" characteristics. The top five characteristics disclosed showed that librarians were thought to be:

* 1) Quiet * 2) Mean or stern * 3) Single/unmarried * 4) Stuffy * 5) In glasses[2]

More than 30 years later, one only has to browse Wikipedia to find that this perception has changed little in the intervening years.

Librarians in popular culture . . . "Stereotypes of librarians in popular culture are frequently negative: librarians are portrayed as puritanical, punitive, unattractive, and introverted if female, or timid, unattractive, and effeminate if male."[3]

In 2007, *The Hollywood Librarian: A Look at Librarians through Film*, a full-length documentary film that focused on the work and lives of librarians, was released.

Using the entertaining and appealing context of American movies, the film holds some surprises for people who may think they know what librarians do. American film contains hundreds of examples of librarians and libraries on screen, some positive, some negative, some laughable and some dead wrong.[4]

Q: Are there school librarians who fit the stereotype?

A: Yes, of course. Nothing can be done about the age, ethnicity, style of hair and/or glasses, and dress of school librarians. If you are female, Caucasian, middle-aged, need glasses to see, and have an appropriate wardrobe for your age and station, there may not be much you can do about it. You fit the physical stereotype of a librarian. However, it is probably unnecessary to wear your hair in a bun, your glasses on a chain sitting on the tip of your nose, and turtlenecks or cardigan sweaters throughout the summer months. One thing you might consider is going to a department store with appropriate accessories. It may be a little more expensive, but it will begin to change your image in the eyes of your students and your fellow teachers. Changing accessories often turns a basic outfit into a stylish one.

Sometimes there is a formal school-wide dress code for teachers and clerical employees, but if there isn't, what is appropriate for librarians? Should male librarians wear a tie? Should librarians adopt a uniform, such as a lab coat, to distinguish themselves from others on campus? The work itself requires a fair amount of sitting, standing, bending, carrying, pushing, and climbing. While this is inconsistent with wearing stilettos and short skirts, it is also not necessary to leave your style at home. Unless you wear a school uniform, which makes dressing a breeze, you have plenty of choices about the image you project with your wardrobe. Whether you are a professional teacher-librarian or a paraprofessional library aide, library clerk, or library media technician, it is in your own best interest to dress in a manner that commands the level of respect you desire. Take your cues from your principal. You should not be dressed more formally. Similarly, if your principal wears suits, you wouldn't want to be wearing jeans and a tank top.

Dos:

- Wear clothing appropriate to the job, especially in terms of comfort and safety.
- Arrive for work clean and groomed.
- Dress up if you expect respect from students and staff.
- Wear clothing that is in good repair, without holes, rips, or stains.
- Keep your nails clean, your breath fresh, and your body odor nonexistent.
- Limit your jewelry, makeup, and fragrance.

Don'ts:

- Look sloppy or overly casual—both give the impression that you don't care.
- Wear flip-flops and cut-off shorts (unless you're promoting a beach theme).
- Wear clothing that would be inappropriate for students to wear.
- Wear clothes with political messages, profane language, or images that may offend others.
- Wear clothing that shows more of you than it should; for example, low-cut blouses or low-rise pants that show thong straps.

Stereotypical behaviors of school librarians, however, are much more concerning than looks. On the other hand, these behaviors are also possible to correct. We cannot ignore that some libraries are not well-run. We can cheerlead and point out excellence, but we also need to critique and encourage offenders to get help or leave the profession. Punitive, authoritarian librarians who demand absolute quiet create an empire with inflexible rules and policies and generally make the library experience excruciating; they are a threat to the future of school libraries.

Q: What are some behaviors that school librarians exhibit that perpetuate a negative stereotype?

A: The following behaviors are examples:

- Constant shushing
- Humorless, short-tempered, or mean-spirited remarks
- Limiting checkout to such an extent as to render the experience meaningless
- Treating cataloging or library tasks as more important than helping patrons
- Refusing help to patrons for a variety of reasons:
  - Because the instructions are written out and patrons need to take personal responsibility
  - Because patrons have already been shown how to do something several times
  - Because patrons have shown poor behavior in the past
  - Because the patron doesn't speak English
  - Because the patron needs information the librarian feels is inappropriate
- Sharing or enforcing judgmental attitudes about what a certain reader should borrow based on "reading level," genre, section, or topic
- Shaming students for forgetting their books or having fines

- Ignoring their privacy by publicly reading off the titles of the books they have checked out if they are overdue
- Sending notices to their parents that list the titles of books (in some states, this is illegal)
- Publicly humiliating students by pointing out things they are checking out, such as easy readers or books on sensitive topics
- Allowing the library to be used as a punishment for offenses that happen elsewhere on campus

Q: How would breaking the stereotype attract patrons?

A: Many people avoid the library because they are afraid of librarians, and unfortunately this may very well begin at a young age. Librarians who truly exhibit the negative behaviors of the stereotype can turn off patrons forever to using libraries of all kinds. This has dramatic implications in an elementary school, where experiences with a bad librarian can influence young students who will then avoid public libraries and libraries in middle school, high school, and college.

Q: How do effective school librarians attract patrons?

- They keep the library open! Students should be able to come to the library during the entire school day and not be turned away for reasons like "another class is visiting" or "your day is Thursday" or "your teacher must bring you with your class." They let students visit before school, during recess, at lunch, during passing periods, and after school. Some librarians go even one step further by keeping school libraries open one night each week, on the weekend, or during extended breaks.
- They schedule special events that connect patrons' interests to the library: author visits, book clubs, movie nights, speakers about high-interest topics, etc.
- They cultivate a welcoming environment where patrons feel safe, accepted, and comfortable. Expectations of library behavior are reasonable, established, and maintained with consistent fairness.
- They provide comfortable seating, studying, and work areas.
- They allow patrons to use technology.

The library must be much more than a book warehouse. The space must be flexible—truly a multipurpose room. "The future library is simultaneously a classroom, computer lab, reading room, study hall, conference center, theater, lecture hall, teacher's lounge, community center (but not a gym), and place for parents to meet" (Meyerberg).[5]

Q: Patrons come in with their class, but I never see them again. How do I make the library "sticky" so that visitors realize that this librarian/library isn't stereotypical?

- Make them know the library is their library.
    - Ask some students to serve on an advisory board to help you improve the library, and then implement their suggestions.
    - Give students an opportunity to make suggestions in a suggestion box.

- Provide access to technology.
  - Are your computers up to date?
  - Are there long lines of people waiting to use a limited number of computers?
  - Do you have to "kick off" patrons who are playing around in favor of those doing "real work"?
  - Are patrons often frustrated when searching for information or trying to access mainstream sites because they are blocked by the filter?
  - Are you or your staff technophobes?
- Ensure caring people are ready to help patrons.
  - This requires continuous training of staff, even if they are student helpers or volunteers.
  - A customer-service attitude is necessary. Remember, they have to come to school, but they often don't have to come to the library.
- Make your library a nice place to spend time. Going to the library shouldn't be a punishment, it should be a reward.
- Keep interesting events happening in the library. Develop a reputation for your library as the place where there is always something to do. Everyone has something they find irresistible, so tap into it.
- Supply a safe haven for students who feel threatened in other environments on campus.
- Develop a collection of quality resources in the appropriate quantity on subjects that are relevant to the interests and needs of students. Try not to judge their choices in literature or topics, and if you are appalled by what they choose to read—keep it to yourself.

Q: Even the other teachers on campus have preconceptions about how I will behave, so how can I overcome this and attract teachers to the library? What keeps them coming back?

- Make their prep easier by having resources for common topics and the standards they are teaching.
- Offer to teach (or better yet, co-teach) the research process.
- Help them find the resources they need when they visit.
- Create wish lists based on resources they are unable to find.
- Inform them when you get quality resources they wouldn't otherwise find.
- Make the library more like a bookstore. Shelve cover out and create attractive display tables.
- Student achievement is the ultimate goal; the librarian committed to helping teachers reach this common goal and overcome challenges will have a bond.
- Develop a collection of exceptional teacher resources, especially literature guides, teacher units, realia, and multimedia. Check your copyright dates. Is everything old and outdated?
- Check your work area and work materials. Do you have a copier, book stapler, electric hole puncher, electric pencil sharpener, paper cutter, die cuts, and meeting space for teams of teachers?
- Depending on the layout of your campus and the personalities of your faculty, you might become the place to go before school (for coffee and cookies), during breaks (to grab a quick book), or after school (to decompress).

Once you have scored your facility, programs, service, and yourself, you need to make one last assessment. Decide if your program provides a twenty-first-century approach. Hopefully you will be able to look through more than your own eyes, but as others see you. Once you have completed this, you can develop your plans to improve their vision of your services.

In the next chapter, you will be able to score how you interACT with your colleagues and staff. This will include how your presence outside the library adds to the image of the library in the education of students.

Notes

1. Hayakawa, S. I. "Recognizing Stereotypes as Substitutes for Thought." *The English Journal* 38(3)(1949): 155–156.

2. Walker, S. and Lawson, V. L. "The Librarian Stereotype and the Movies." *MC Journal: The Journal of Academic Media Librarianship* 1(1)(1993): 16–28.

3. Wikipedia, http://en.wikipedia.org/wiki/Librarians_in_popular_culture Accessed April 14, 2010.

4. Kniffel, L. "Hollywood Librarian vs. Real Thing." *American Libraries* 36 (6)(2005): 22.

5. Meyerberg, H. "School Libraries: A Design Recipe for the Future." *Knowledge Quest* 31(1)(2002): 11–13.

CHAPTER 4

The InterACTive Librarian

Most libraries have enough behind-the-scenes work to keep school librarians busy, but you need to be interacting with teachers, students, and parents for your true value to be known. Sometimes it may feel like you need to be 10 places at once, but that just shows that you are connected to the other people and events happening on campus.

Ten "InterACTion" Action Items for Every School Librarian

Do:

✓ Make sure you have a presence at every faculty meeting
✓ Know what is happening elsewhere in the school regardless if it affects the library
✓ Eat lunch with others on campus—don't isolate yourself
✓ Provide reports about library programs and services to your principal and the PTA
✓ Attend meetings of library staff within your district (or if they don't happen, start these meetings)
✓ Show up at big school events: Back-to-School Night, Open House, and Homecoming
✓ Volunteer to sit on key committees: Technology, Curriculum, and Safety
✓ Join the PTA
✓ Continue learning—attend professional growth days, conferences, or take that next step for another degree
✓ Maintain a membership in one or more professional associations: the State Library Association or State School Library Association, the American Association of School Librarians, and the American Library Association

Our definitions:

interact: School library staff works together, provides service to patrons, and collaborates with others. *It is often hard for librarians to interact with the rest of the teachers because they are busy running the library.*

interaction: Exchange of information, ideas, and opinions between and among learners and teachers, sometimes occurring through technology with the aim of facilitating learning. *The interaction with our librarian is an important part of our school's success in implementing professional learning communities.*

interactive:

1. Two-way, the school library and its patrons are capable of acting on or influencing each other. *The librarian's interactive style made students comfortable asking more questions.*
2. Synergistic, the school library staff and patrons working together so the total effect is greater than the sum of the two (or more) participants. *My first year teaching was difficult, but the librarian made it so much easier with an interactive unit on a research project for my senior students.*
3. The ability for patrons to "converse," either physically or virtually, with school library staff where questions, feedback, and responses occur. *The 24/7 interactive "Ask a Librarian" saved me last night when I was up until midnight finishing my paper.*
4. Providing output to school library users based on their input, which feeds back into the user's decision process for subsequent interaction. *The new interactive library catalog is awesome because I can send recommendations to the librarian about books to buy for our library.*
5. Implying that the school library patron can exert some control over the environment and services and not just be a passive recipient. *Interactive story time lets the librarian pick audience members who continue the story after he starts it.*

True or Not-So-True Quiz

Read each statement and think about how you would answer the related questions. Use the following scale to rate your responses.

Scale: 5 = True without exception; 4 = Mostly true; 3 = Sometimes true; 2 = Rarely true; 1 = Never true

1. _____ Interacting with students and teachers recharges my internal battery.
   - How tired am I when I leave work?
   - Do I leave the minute my "time is served?"
   - Do I feel relieved when teachers "forget" to come or cancel a visit?

2. _____ I can leave the library to attend meetings, collaborate with teachers, and interact with others.
   - Am I the only person in the library?
   - Do I have to lock the door when I leave?

- Do I have to take breaks and eat lunch in the library so it can remain open?
- Do I choose to remain in the library because I am completely absorbed or enjoying it too much to leave?

3. _____ I encourage volunteers to work in the library.
   - Are parent volunteers present often?
   - Do student volunteers make a significant contribution?
   - Have I given up on trying to have volunteer help because of reliability and quality-control issues?

4. _____ I praise excellence when I see it on campus with students, teachers, and others.
   - Am I so absorbed with what is happening in the library that I couldn't point out the excellent work of others?
   - Am I insecure about other programs taking the limelight, such as the computer lab, the art and music program, or the homework club?
   - Do I make note of the programs and clubs that are thriving to inform collection development?

5. _____ I broadcast library programs that are successful and toot my own horn.
   - Am I too modest to point out what I do when my efforts are going unnoticed?
   - Am I too busy inside the library to attend occasions (PTA meetings, staff meetings, or celebrations) where I might talk about the library and my role?
   - Do I regularly contribute news for the daily announcements or newsletter?

6. _____ I enjoy socializing with my coworkers and attend events where I have the chance to speak to decision-makers.
   - Do I isolate myself from others on campus because I need peace and quiet?
   - Am I uncomfortable spending time with others on campus because we have nothing in common?
   - Do I eat lunch or take breaks at the same time as my colleagues?
   - Do I attend social events when I'm invited; baby showers, weddings, candle parties, staff holiday or year-end parties, bunko, and/or book clubs?

7. _____ I am confident that my presence is needed and appreciated on campus.
   - Do I get thank-you notes, cards, or token gifts from my administrator, teaching staff, or students?
   - Do teachers value their library time for more than just a break from active teaching?
   - Do students come to the library for academic and research help, to study, to work on projects with peers, or to read?
   - Do students ever come just to have a conversation or confide in someone who cares?
   - Do students look at the library as a place they like to be, whether they are studying, researching, relaxing, or visiting for pleasure?

8. _____ Working with children and teachers is the best part of my job.
   - Would I be happier if I could just close the library for a few weeks and concentrate on cataloging, inventory, or fixing bulletin boards?
   - Is my favorite time when the library is empty and I can focus on putting books back on the shelves and straightening everything?

- Would I jump at the chance to have a change of position where I could provide support services to librarians instead of to patrons?
- Am I more interested in planning the lesson then actually teaching it?

9. _____ I am ready to showcase my library should the superintendent and/or school board members chance to drop by for a tour.
   - Would I be flustered if the library didn't appear to be perfectly kept: books sitting on book carts, stacked on counters, the book drop full, materials strewn about room, or books falling over on the shelves?
   - Would I begin shushing the students, shooing out patrons, and subverting the usual chaos in the room?
   - Would I feel appalled if there was a lack of activity in the room, especially if this persisted for the entire length of the visit?

10. _____ I feel empowered and proficient when a teacher asks to collaborate with me.
    - Do I have areas where I should have expertise but don't?
    - Am I bashful about my teaching skills? Is it easier for me to instruct students when the teacher is not present?
    - Is my schedule so packed that I discourage teachers from approaching me on projects that will be time consuming for me?

11. _____ I am in tune with the activities and interests of the students. I participate in discussions with them about the sports, hobbies, TV shows, movies, games, and music they enjoy.
    - Do I think that the current generation of students is inferior to previous ones? Do I feel that students have changed? Do I perceive them as disrespectful, selfish, or lazy?
    - Do I have disdain for everything about popular culture?
    - Am I unlikely to purchase materials that students want to read in favor of things I think they ought to be reading?

12. _____ I am abreast of the curriculum that the teachers use, the standards that they teach, and the pressures they are under.
    - Would I be completely lost if I was asked to cover for another teacher for any length of time?
    - Can I find resources for teachers based on the standard they are teaching?
    - Do I offer to help out during those crunch times of report-card deadlines, periods of intensive testing and grading, or parent-teacher conferences?

13. _____ I am comfortable asking the students, teachers, principal, and PTA for things I need.
    - Am I afraid to ask for anything for the library?
    - Do I involve the teachers in the library, allowing them to help by checking books in, putting books back on the shelf, or assisting patrons who need help?
    - Do I let the students "take over" the library and pay for it later when they leave it a disaster?

14. _____ I do not take it personally when people criticize the library program or request changes.
    - Have I built a personal empire that doesn't fit the needs of the school?
    - Have I created policies that restrict the options of patrons to make my job easier, such as one-book limits, only allowing them to choose books from the return cart, or off of tables instead of shelves?

- Do criticisms simply deflate my plans to start anything new? Does it seem like nothing is good enough or appreciated?
- When others ask about my job, am I more likely to say something positive or deflect criticism by pointing out the things that are wrong and offering excuses?

15. _____ I am a valued member of campus groups. I am asked to serve on committees and attend meetings, and others can count on me to be there and follow through on promises made.
   - Do I overextend myself and end up begging off of commitments?
   - Do I have good intentions but not necessarily the means to make anything happen?
   - Am I perceived by others as someone who "takes over" and micromanages?
   - Is it just easier to do it myself?

Scoring: Add up your scores.
75–70 Interaction is maximized (you probably don't need this book)
69–60 Plenty of healthy interaction
59–45 Adequate interaction, but areas can be targeted for improvement
44–30 Making yourself more interactive needs to become a top priority
29–15 Time to take an assertiveness class

Use the results of the quiz to rate yourself. If you have a very low score, it is probably unrealistic to think that you will become a joiner in a short time. Try setting yourself two actionable goals for improving your score, and start with one of the areas where you scored a 1 or 2. Notice that the questions tend to be related to your personality or things you can change by yourself. Only infrequently are there obstacles where you would need administrative support. Check your answers for questions 2, 12, and 14. If your answers are low, you need to determine if you can fix these on your own or if you'll need your administrator's help.

On the other hand, if the item is primarily or wholly based on your personality, and you gave yourself a low score, it may be that you are not in the right position. Look at your answers for the following questions:

1. _____ 8. _____ 11. _____ Total: _____

If you have low scores on these questions (a total of 7 or less), your chance of having long-term happiness in your career is also low. Are you burned out or simply in the wrong position? Perhaps you should look into providing support services to librarians in another location instead of direct service at the site level.

Personality

The personality types found in library environments (although not specifically school libraries) have been a frequent topic of studies since the

1980s. J. L. Holland, in his theory of career choice, supports the idea that people choose their careers based on the best fit between their own personality and the demands of the career.[1]

Two different studies of librarians and library students used the Myers-Briggs Type Indicator and found similar results.[2,3] Although the participants in the studies scored in all 16 categories on the Myers-Briggs scale, two personality types accounted for about 29 percent of library students and 49 percent of acting librarians. The two types are ISTJ (introverted, sensing, thinking, and judging) and INTJ (introverted, intuitive, thinking, and judging).

ISTJ (Estimated frequency in U.S. population, 11–14 percent)[4]

Quiet, serious, earns success by thoroughness and dependability. Practical, matter-of-fact, realistic, and responsible. Decide logically what should be done and work toward it steadily, regardless of distractions. Take pleasure in making everything orderly and organized—their work, their home, their life. Value traditions and loyalty.

INTJ (Accounts for only 1–4 percent of the general population)[5]
Have original minds and great drive for implementing their ideas and achieving their goals. Quickly see patterns in external events and develop long-range explanatory perspectives. When committed, organize a job and carry it through. Skeptical and independent, have high standards of competence and performance—for themselves and others.
These descriptions and those of the other 14 personality types can be found at The Myers & Briggs Foundation Web site (http://www.myers briggs.org).

Although this study has not been duplicated specifically with *school* librarians, it would not be surprising to find that they and school library paraprofessionals are also typically introverted, organized, logical, committed, and practical. These characteristics are the very qualities that would make them successful in, and perhaps fulfilled by, their daily activities.

Interestingly, Hatchard and Crocker (1990) found that when librarians interact with their patrons, there are three vital characteristics that enhance approachability: friendliness, patience, and helpfulness.[6] These are not the same characteristics that librarians typically exhibit, as referenced by the dominant personality types above. This may be one reason why patrons have an impression of librarians that continues to fit the stereotype.

Knowing your personality type or at least the kind of activities that make you happy is an important step in determining if you are in the right position. This doesn't mean that an introverted person should put on a façade and turn into a social butterfly, but it does mean that school librarians must connect with others even if it isn't comfortable for them. If you are insecure or uneasy when engaging with others in environments outside of the library, such as PTA events, staff meetings, or school board meetings, a good first step is to simply show up. After you have attended a number of meetings and have quietly observed the rules and interactions that are normal for that group, you will become more comfortable contributing. Sharing the good news about what is happening in the library doesn't have to come off as bragging, but more like passing on information in the form of results. Tell the stories of the successes of teachers and students, and don't downplay the importance of your role and that of the library.

Isolation and the Effect on School Librarians

Isolation is a common complaint of many school librarians. Regardless of the status or position held, school librarians and paraprofessionals alike are often trapped alone in the library providing service that no one else understands. No one else on campus is available with whom to commiserate, brainstorm, share the workload, or collaborate about managing the library. Additionally, school library personnel often report to a site administrator who has no background or training in librarianship. While there are other education professionals on campus, they are focused on what is happening in their classrooms or within their specialty.

Keeping up with the best practices, trends, and issues in school libraries can be difficult for school librarians who see only what is happening on their own campus or in their own school district. Mary Ann Harlan's *Personal Learning Networks: Professional Development for the Isolated School Librarian* (2009) describes ways to reduce isolation through technology and professional association membership.[7] Social technologies, such as blogs, wikis, webinars, interactive tutorials, and teleconferencing, are described as ways to break out of this isolation and connect with other school librarians. One library blogger posted this comment: "Librarian blogging combats isolation, offering a way to share ideas and issues with like-minded colleagues without geographic or time constraints."[8]

Mentoring programs have sprung up in response to the isolation factor for school library personnel. The New Jersey Association of School Libraries points to the lack of easily obtainable help for those new to the profession and profound feelings of isolation as reasons for developing a mentoring handbook and matching newcomers to those with experience.[9]

Don't forget, too, that public librarians, especially if they specialize in children's or young adult services, are a good place to start if no other network is available. Public librarians have many areas of overlapping concern, and mutually beneficial programs can occur through effective public library/school library collaborations.

Meetings in Schools

Meetings are time consuming, and often it is difficult to see that any benefit comes from the time spent. However, they are a fact of life in most institutions and must be dealt with by everyone working there. Sometimes, they are required, leaving you no choice. At other times, the decision is yours.

Why attend meetings?

- It shows that you care about and are committed to the school.
- It keeps you accountable for accomplishing tasks that affect other entities.
- It builds relationships with other meeting participants, many of whom have influence with decision-makers and other groups.
- It allows you to have a voice in a wide variety of ways: voting, debating, and offering background and expertise.
- It raises the profile of the school library through your involvement.

Too many meetings occur on campus for you to attend all of them, and in fact you can become so bogged down with meetings that you can't get anything else done. However, there are a few meetings that you must attend if you want to be visible and knowledgeable about what is happening on campus.

Teaching-Staff Meetings

You need to attend meetings of the teaching staff and should not ask your administrator to give you permission to miss them. When you, a certified school library "teacher," do not attend these meetings, it is easier for other teachers to dismiss you as less than a real teacher. Even if you only sit quietly and observe, it is impossible not to network with those around you eventually. Building a network of colleagues and professional acquaintances can be especially important when the time comes to prioritize services and the staff is allowed to vote for something that affects you or the library. If there are staff members whom you may otherwise never see, it is much easier for them to vote for an elimination of library services if they have never seen or met you.

Thus, teaching-staff meetings are also where administrative directives are generally announced, and it is important that you hear it in the same time and place as all the other teachers. Practical, everyday details will be relayed that are important, such as deadlines, budgets, test scores, expectations, and announcements. Hearing it secondhand from others introduces the concern that it is reported to you inaccurately. You want to make your own judgments as to how a pronouncement affects the library and ask how certain edicts pertain to you.

In addition to library issues, you should speak up when things don't seem right. You may be able to offer essential information about copyright, fair use, and plagiarism issues that keep the school safe legally. You also need to be there for other serendipitous occasions when you are the one who can offer information, answers, or expertise to the whole staff. If the library is to be the heart of the school, you need to be the pacemaker at those meetings.

Additionally, these meetings allow you to observe the culture of the school. Only through careful observation at these meetings can you determine the power players, the pot stirrers, the off-topic meeting disrupters, and the shining stars. When you need others to support your cause, you want to align yourself with those who effect change. The polite, friendly teacher who comes to the library and visits pleasantly with you could turn out to be the last person you want representing library issues because he or she is viewed as a malcontent who casts every issue as a crisis.

Believe it or not, you may actually end up looking forward to teaching-staff meetings because it reduces the isolation of being in the library. It gives you opportunities to find out what others are teaching and to offer collaborative support. Over time, you will build a group of teacher friends who become school library advocates. You need this collegial support to help you achieve goals for an exceptional library program.

One effective means of making sure teachers and administrators are given an opportunity to visit the library regularly is to invite the principal to hold the faculty meeting in the library. If you volunteered to hold the first teaching-staff meeting of the year in the library and provided cookies and coffee, it could start a trend, with other teachers bringing snacks for other meetings. While they are in the library, they will observe bulletin boards, displays, and other evidence of the relationship of the library in the lives of students.

Parent-Teacher Organizations

Whether the group that meets on your campus is part of the national PTA or PTSA (allowing student membership) or is a stand-alone PTO, it is important that you become a member. The dues are usually affordable, and it allows you to attend and vote at meetings. Attend enough meetings that you are known to the group, and consider taking a leadership position if you have time. The parent-teacher organization will almost always advocate for and fund your library program. Parents quickly learn that the library is there to support the literacy and academic efforts of their children. Maintaining a positive relationship with parents increases the chance that they will participate and help you with fund-raisers. They may also maintain line items in their budget to support collection development, program sponsorship, reading incentives, or even salaries. You might even pick up some volunteers to help in the library.

School Site Council

The school site council (SSC) consists of teachers, parents, and classified employees (and occasionally students and community members) who work with the principal to develop, review, and evaluate school improvement programs and school budgets. Their peers generally elect the members of the SSC; this means that a school librarian wishing to serve will need to get the votes of the rest of the teachers. Additionally, library paraprofessionals may serve as classified employees and have a significant effect on funding.

The exact duties of the SSC vary from state to state and even between districts in the same state. Generally, they advise the principal on specific school budget decisions and the academic plan.

Although the PTA can have a substantial impact on school library funding by way of donations, the SSC deals with school policy and budgets. Serving as a council member can mean brief meetings once a month serving as a de facto rubber stamp or at most advising the principal without authority to enforce decisions. However, there are schools where SSCs are powerful and have the last word on staffing and budgetary decisions, including evaluating the principal and hiring teachers. On this type of SSC, these are highly competitive positions of significant influence that entail extensive meetings, additional formal training to understand the categorical programs, the role of the council, and the required plan components. Most site councils defer to the principal's professional judgment, but there are situations in which participants become actively involved in developing new programs or overseeing major school changes.

Grade Level or Departmental Meetings

Depending on the structure of your school, there are generally teams of teachers that meet regularly to plan instruction or coordinate with one another on a variety of issues. These can be high-performing teams that share virtually all aspects of instruction or loosely knit groups that simply meet on a regular basis as required by the administration. Regardless, offer yourself as a resource if you are able. You may have expertise for this group or find out about collaborative opportunities by attending. Getting an invitation to one of these meetings can be accomplished by approaching your administrator or the leader of that group, perhaps a department chair, and asking if there is a way that you could come to listen or give some pertinent information to the group. These meetings may turn into a gold mine of opportunities or they may not pan out, but reaching out to subgroups within your school is another way to increase your visibility.

Committees

Teachers and classified staff never lack committee opportunities, and you may be asked to participate. These committees can be important or inconsequential, so choosing the right ones takes time and experience. Usually there are key committees that command the interest of the administrator:

• Academics/curriculum
• Budget

- Safety
- Staff development
- Student behavior
- Technology

These committees might be formed by appointment, election, or simply by asking for volunteer members. Generally, the committees that matter to the administration are the ones that are mandated by a school charter, single school plan, or education code, but administrators also have special interests and may need to create ad hoc committees that hold great significance.

Do not ignore other committee opportunities that present themselves. School librarians can be valuable members of any committee when they have genuine interest or enthusiasm. The following is a list of examples not meant to be all-inclusive:

- Advisory
  - Advanced placement
  - District
  - English learners
  - Gifted and talented
  - Special education
- Assessment/testing
- Awards/recognition
- Communication
  - Newsletter
  - Web site
- Diversity
- Facilities
- Social
  - Celebrations
  - Events
  - Sunshine
- Student activities
  - Athletics
  - Prom
- Research
- Wellness
  - Fitness
  - Health
  - Nutrition

If you do not have a library committee at your school, it is in your best interest to start one! This can be an advisory board made up of parents, teachers, students, and yourself. This may be a required component of an officially adopted school library plan, or simply a way for you to connect with stakeholders. You should have a nominated and elected chairperson who will run your meetings, and you should take an active and interested role.

A final note about committee meetings: be careful not to spread yourself too thin. Unless you are specifically assigned to committees by your administrator, be careful not to join too many. You can easily become overcommitted to committee work and end up wanting to be committed!

Library Meetings

Assuming your district or area has regular meetings for school librarians, your attendance is critical. System-wide meetings allow all the people with similar jobs to get together and discuss issues, concerns, and practical details. It is best when the meetings are coordinated by someone who understands the work and the needs of the school librarians, such as a director of media services, a library coordinator, or a district librarian, but if this is not the case, the library community should elect one representative to follow through on unresolved items. These meetings should have an agenda so that they don't devolve into gripe sessions that aren't productive. If there is a negative connotation at these meetings, make it a regular practice to bring at least one positive example of the difference the school library is making for student achievement. If you have experience, reach out to newcomers and help them develop a positive attitude.

Don't forget vertical relationships. Elementary school librarians need to talk to middle/intermediate/junior high school librarians and vice versa. K–8 librarians need to connect with high school librarians. High school librarians should be connecting with community college librarians. The feeder school librarians can learn a lot about the success of their programs by listening to the concerns about incoming students as they enter the next level of education. How else will you know if your efforts are providing students with the skills they need to be successful throughout their academic careers? These relationships can pay off dividends later should your position be threatened. For example, if a school librarian position is proposed for elimination, a very powerful message to the school board might come from a community college librarian describing the negative impact to students who will not be ready for a college experience

Don't limit yourself to networking just with people in your own district, though. Try to branch out by attending professional-development activities at a local level, whether provided by your district or a county office of education, and in some states there are regional centers with people who can be helpful. The department of education in your state or another nearby library system will have persons who can offer assistance.

If you are pursuing a library-related degree, you'll meet fellow librarians in your classes. Even if you've finished your formal education, check your community college offerings or pursue university extension classes to stay current and keep your repertoire growing. Many classes are now provided online so you aren't limited by geography. If these opportunities don't lure you, keep your eyes open for seminars that come near you through organizations such as the Bureau of Educational Research (BER) that have several strands for library media educators.[10]

You may get mail from organizations such as California's Infopeople staff which offers low-cost or free seminars for all types of libraries.[11] Several divisions of the American Library Association now offer virtual workshops, which you can attend, although the cost is often higher for nonmembers.

Another source may be your vendors, who are invested in making sure that you understand how to use and maximize the importance of their product. The library software that you use to catalog and circulate your collection often has additional features (perhaps at an extra cost) that enhance the library user's experience. It is important to at least know what those features include.

Professional Associations

Join!

You must first belong and attend functions to get the full benefits of membership. You should be a member of professional library associations to network and keep abreast. You can join one or all of these groups, but you will get the most out of your efforts if you regularly attend their events and read the information they provide by way of journals and newsletters. You will truly benefit most if you get involved through volunteering for the governance of these organizations. The connections you make with people across the state and country who believe in the same things that you do cannot be overstated.

The International Association of School Librarianship (IASL) has a global perspective. The organization communicates primarily through its electronic newsletter and Web sites. Countries are divided into zones, with the United States, Australia, Canada, and most European countries in Zone A. Most countries also have their own national school library association.

In the United States, school librarians should join the American Association of School Libraries (AASL), and you'll also belong to the American Library Association (ALA). You'll receive a subscription to *Knowledge Quest*, a bimonthly publication during the school year, and a monthly e-mail newsletter called *AASL Hotlinks*. AASL has a conference every two years, and the ALA meets twice annually, in the mid-winter for business meetings and in the summer for its full-blown conference.

Check chapter 2 for your state school library association and be sure to join it and attend its events. Consider joining the state library association, too, especially if your state does not have a separate association for school libraries. There are also regional associations, such as the New England School Library Association.

Many states have local library associations that you can join. In Nevada, the Clark County School Librarians Association is a grassroots organization dedicated to the hundreds of school library media specialists just within that district.

Other organizations in which school librarians have a significant interest in belonging include Computer-Using Educators (CUE) and the International Society for Technology in Education (ISTE). Both have special interest groups for school librarians because technology and library media services intersect. Other organizations with overlap include reading associations and a variety of literacy groups.

Your skills in making your presence known outside the library as well as your expertise in managing what goes on within its walls means you have met your colleagues in the lunchroom, been visible at big school events, worked on committees, and joined and participated with the parent-teacher association. You have exercised your professional obligation to join your professional association. You are now ready to look at your collaboration score.

Notes

1. Rybash, J. M., Roodin, P. A., and Hoyer, W. J. *Adult Development and Aging*, 3rd Edition. Boston: McGraw-Hill, 1995.

2. Agada, J. "Profiling Librarians with the Myers-Briggs Type Indicator: Studies in Self Selection and Type Stability." *Education for Information* (16) (March 1998): 57–69.

3. Scherdin, M. J., and Beaubien, A. "Shattering Our Stereotype: Librarians' New Image." *Library Journal* (12) (July 1995): 35–38.

4. Center for Applications of Psychological Type, http://www.capt.org/mbti-assessment/estimated-frequencies.htm. Accessed November 24, 2009.

5. Center for Applications of Psychological Type, http://www.capt.org/mbti-assessment/estimated-frequencies.htm. Accessed November 24, 2009.

6. Hatchard, D. B., and Crocker, C. "Library Users—A Psychological Profile." *Australian Academic and Research Libraries* 21 (2) (1990): 97–105.

7. Harlan, M. A. *Personal Learning Networks: Professional Development for the Isolated School Librarian*. Englewood, CO: Libraries Unlimited, 2009.

8. Alice in Infoland, http://www.aliceinfo.org/, March 29, 2007, posting. Accessed November 24, 2009.

9. New Jersey Association of School Librarians, http://www.njasl.org/documents/NJASLMentoringHandbook.pdf (2007). Accessed November 23, 2009.

10. Bureau of Educational Research Web site, http://www.ber.org/. Accessed November 24, 2009.

11. Infopeople, http://infopeople.org. Accessed November 24, 2009.

CHAPTER 5

The CollaborACTive Librarian

Working with others on important tasks is an essential part of academic life. This chapter gives you ideas for building relationships with others so that collaboration can prosper. While school librarians and teachers in the same building can easily meet face to face, it is increasingly easier to connect with others outside your campus via electronic media such as e-mail, teleconferencing, and Web 2.0 collaborative tools.

Ten "Collaboration" Action Items for Every School Librarian

Do:

✓ Find out who the contact person is at your closest public library branch and suggest holding a meeting
✓ Reach out to teachers or departments where assistance would be natural and helpful (for example, fifth-grade state reports, history/social science research papers, science research, or genre studies in English/language arts)
✓ Have something ready to hand to any teacher who wants to collaborate—make sure it is easy and quick for them to fill out and understand.
✓ Collect work samples to show interested teachers so they don't have to "reinvent the wheel"
✓ Understand inquiry-based learning and feel prepared to help students complete these types of activities
✓ Send out an invitation to collaborate and attach something "sweet," maybe chocolate, to pique their interest
✓ Look at your schedule—if you have a fixed-block schedule, try to find some time (even if it is 20 minutes a day) that you can reserve for collaborative teaching
✓ Attend the staff development days with the teachers, even if you don't think it applies to you—you will make connections between what they are trying to achieve and what you have to offer in the library

✓ Find out if your administrator is a supporter of collaboration—Will it be encouraged or frowned upon? Will it be celebrated or silenced? Can your administrator set the tone by recommending it to departments? Will your administrator support a flexible (or more flexible) schedule?

✓ Remember your library colleagues. Do you meet with others who do the same job within your district or area? Investigate the idea of sharing information about successful collaborations. Regularly contribute templates and instruction sheets that will encourage others to replicate successful projects.

Our definitions:

collaborate: School librarians join forces with classroom teachers and others on campus to work toward individual and common goals. *School librarians are able to provide expertise and resources to classroom teachers and collaborate on something that would be too large for them to accomplish alone.*

collaboration:

1. The act of working jointly in a recursive process toward an intersection of common goals. *Collaboration allows teachers and school librarians to jointly teach the research process and content at the same time.*
2. The process in which two or more individuals work together to integrate information in order to enhance student learning. *Collaboration allows teachers and school librarians to decrease the student-teacher ratio.*

collaborative: An intellectual endeavor that is creative in nature: sharing knowledge, learning, and building consensus. *The public library-school library collaborative benefits not only the students, but also the programs at both institutions.*

Collaboration Quiz

Reflect on your best collaborative effort and choose the option that most closely resembles the results you achieved. If you haven't had an opportunity to collaborate, which one would be most comfortable for you to try the first time?

1. Who initiated the project?
   A. I did.
   B. The teacher did.
   C. We casually both came up with the idea.
   D. The principal or another administrator told us we had to.
   E. The grade-level team or department requested it.

2. Who designed the assignments and/or activities?
   A. I did.
   B. The teacher did.
   C. We both participated in creating it.
   D. We used the adopted curriculum or materials created by others.

E. We used both the adopted text and supplemented with library materials and electronic resources.

3. Who taught the content?
   A. I did.
   B. The teacher did.
   C. We both participated in teaching the content.
   D. The students each studied a part of the content and then taught each other during presentations.
   E. The students learned the content from the activities they were assigned; no whole group direct instruction was necessary.

4. Who taught the process?
   A. I did.
   B. The teacher did.
   C. We both participated in teaching the process.
   D. There wasn't any time to teach the process so I worked with small groups when I could.
   E. The students learned the process from the activities that they were designed for them to complete, although some coaching was necessary when teams hit roadblocks.

5. Who was the expert?
   A. I was.
   B. The teacher was.
   C. I was the expert regarding the process, and the teacher was the expert about the students and the content.
   D. The students didn't need an expert because the activities could be completed without assistance.
   E. We brought in an outside expert to engage the students, and complemented one another by applying our expertise about the content, students, and library as needed.

6. How many meetings did it take before you were ready to begin?
   A. Just one quick meeting.
   B. The teacher came and told me what should be done.
   C. We met several times in person and both contributed ideas.
   D. We never met, I just e-mailed my ideas and the teacher told me to go with it.
   E. We met several times over a series of weeks to complete at least two of the following: to plan, to evaluate the progress, to assess student work, or to evaluate the final results.

7. Who graded the student work?
   A. I did.
   B. The teacher did.
   C. We each gave a grade to the same assignment: one for content and one for process and form.
   D. I graded the work I assigned, and the teacher graded the work assigned in the classroom.
   E. We didn't assign a letter grade, but allowed teams to self-assess and give feedback to other groups; it was an experience rather than an assessment opportunity.

8. Were you able to measure the effect of your participation?
   A. Yes, the entire work was attributable to me.
   B. No, I wasn't a part of the grading.
   C. Yes, we were able to take the work product scores and compare them to a similar group of students who completed the project without library support.
   D. No, the grade and assignment were not conducive to determining if the library support helped students; this project could have been completed in the classroom alone.
   E. Yes and no; there wasn't a comparison group, but the students' work was exceptional and they reported that they were more confident in the research process with library support.

9. Are there any artifacts or student work samples that you can use to showcase this project?
   A. Yes, the work is displayed in the library.
   B. No, all the work was returned to the teacher and/or students.
   C. Yes, some of the work is displayed in the library, and students gave permission to make copies of outstanding examples.
   D. No, the work they completed was done poorly and wouldn't impress anyone to work with me.
   E. Yes, the work is in electronic format and is posted, with permission, to our library Web site.

10. Is this teacher likely to approach you about a future collaboration using the same project?
    A. Yes, it was a nice break for the teacher and provided lots of prep time.
    B. No, but the teacher seemed really happy with the student learning and results and indicated an interest in doing it again next year in the classroom.
    C. Yes, and now I have to do it with all the teachers in that grade or subject area!
    D. No, it took too much time and the teacher indicated that the results weren't worth all the effort.
    E. Yes, but we're going to tweak it to make it even better.

Tally up your answers!

A:_____   B: _____   C: _____   D: _____   E: _____

Interpreting: *Look at the areas in which most of your answers fell.*

A: You were largely responsible for planning and delivering instruction, and the success is directly attributable to you. The teacher's contribution was little or nothing, so this might not really be an example of collaboration, but more "borrowing" the students for some library learning.

B: You allowed the teacher to plan and deliver instruction and gave limited support when the class actually visited the library. Although you could count this as collaboration, the teacher is likely to think of this more as a library visit and not something that the two of you did together.

C: These indicate true collaboration with clearly defined roles so that both part-ners were contributing. Not only was this an effective collaboration, but the results showed significant student learning.

D: This indicates a collaboration gone wrong! The students didn't take it seriously, the teacher didn't seem interested, and the students weren't doing any signifi-cant learning of either content or process.

E: The assignments used were most likely inquiry-based learning projects, and the deliverable project that the students created probably required them to learn something new about technology as well. These results can be used to promote further collaborations and, more importantly, to showcase the importance of the library to the school and to the academic success of all students.

Why Collaborate?

Teachers may not understand the role of collaboration in the education of students. When the emphasis is being placed on test scores to assess stu-dent achievement and even merit-pay increases, many teachers close their doors so their students can concentrate on preparing for tests. This makes it a challenge to answer the question "Why collaborate?" and to convince teachers and administrators that collaboration can help them teach and help students learn. Some reasons you might offer include:

• The number of students from diverse backgrounds who demonstrate low or fail-ing test scores is growing.
• Schools are operating with diminishing resources: fewer support staff, outdated technology, and larger class sizes.
• The explosion of information, especially available electronically, has created a more complex learning environment.
• Standards-based education requires creative ways of meeting prescribed out-comes while engaging students in meaningful learning experiences.

Public Library and School Library Collaboration

The public library and the school library do not have the same purpose or goals, but there is some overlap. A few of the commonalities are to:

• Introduce, promote, and encourage children to love and appreciate reading and good literature.
• Develop capable, critical users of information and technology.
• Assist children in understanding themselves and their world.
• Encourage children to develop to their fullest potential.
• Develop lifelong learners.

How can librarians from each organization help and support one another? First there must be communication between the public library and school library about the strengths and weaknesses of each organization.

When one organization has an obstacle, the other can step in and supply that missing piece. Four examples follow.

Scenario 1: A goal of the school library media program is to provide instruction in information and research skills using information technology.

Obstacle: The school library cannot afford to purchase the databases and electronic resources that would support teaching these skills.

Solution: The students can use the public library resources as long as they have a public library card.

School librarian's role: Distribute library card applications and plan a field trip for the class to the public library, collect completed applications and forward them to the public librarian prior to the class visit, and schedule a block of time for the public librarian to visit the school to train the students to use the electronic resources via the school library computers.

Public librarian's role: Conduct a library tour when the class comes to visit on a field trip, have library cards ready to distribute when students arrive, and travel to the school to make a presentation to the class about logging on to the public library Web site using the tools within via their school or home.

Scenario 2: A goal of the public library is to assist students with homework assignments.

Obstacle: Public librarians do not have advance notice of assignments and therefore do not have resources set aside, or the students get stuck because they didn't bring their textbooks.

Solution: Establish multiple paths for teachers to easily inform the public library of assignments, especially those where students are likely to need public library services. House reference copies of current textbooks at the public library.

School librarian's role: Provide one copy of each textbook, taking into consideration space and frequency of need at the public library. Pass out several copies of the form the public librarian provides to teachers and tell them how public librarians use it to help students with their assignments. Encourage them to use these forms—maybe give them chocolate! Have teachers turn these forms in to the school library; it will be useful information there, too. Forward them to the public library. If possible, have an electronic system so that teachers can do this online. Demonstrate for the teachers how easy it is to do at a staff meeting or department meeting. Homework assignments that are posted on the library or school Web site might also be posted on the public library's Web site if the information is provided in advance.

Public librarian's role: Create and distribute forms that are quick and easy for teachers to fill out, but also capture the information needed. When forms are received, send a confirmation notice to the teachers so that they know the information provided was helpful. If possible, send a follow-up note after the due date as to the number of students that were helped.

Scenario 3: A goal of the public library is to have a thriving summer reading program. A goal of the school library is to have students continue to read all summer long even though the school library is closed.

Obstacle: Parents and schoolchildren aren't aware of the summer reading program or do not participate because of challenges related to public library hours and transportation. The school librarian is not funded in the summer and the school library is locked.

Solution: School and public librarians actively promote the programs on the school campus to both students and parents. If the students can't come to the public library, bring the program to them. Offer it as a club after summer-school dismissal or through the school's extended child care program.

School librarian's role: Dedicate one bulletin board to the summer reading program beginning in April. Use the theme and materials provided by the public librarian. Set aside a day, or days, when the public librarian can come to the school to talk up the program to the students and answer their questions either in the library during visits, at small assemblies, or in classrooms. Make sure that you get flyers and other printed information approved for distribution ahead of time, if necessary. Invite the public librarians to set up a table during an open house or other event when parents will be on campus. Set up a meeting between the child care program leader and the public librarian to form a plan for conducting the summer reading program at the school site.

Public librarian's role: Provide the summer reading program theme and supplemental materials to the school librarian in March. Coordinate with the school librarian to make school visits to promote the program and answer student questions. Make sure that you get flyers and other printed information approved for distribution ahead of time, if necessary. Set up a table during open house to promote the program to parents who may not be aware of it. Meet with the child care program leader to coordinate running an "off-site" summer reading program, perhaps with a drop collection that you rotate weekly or a weekly prize distribution for readers.

Scenario 4: A goal of both libraries is to have materials and resources sufficient to the needs of the patrons.

Obstacle: The school library budget may not allow for purchasing multiple copies of highly requested titles. The public library may not stock a variety of titles in the children's nonfiction section that are in high demand when teachers assign similar projects.

Solution: Institute an interlibrary loan plan. Work out the details so that the possible loss of materials is evenly distributed and minimized.

Roles: The person responsible for library services at the school district level must work with the appropriate person at the public library to make an ambitious program like this succeed. The coordination needed will require a formal, written commitment from both parties.

A multitude of ways is available for collaboration between the public and school libraries that will benefit students, teachers, and families. Remember, too, that this is a piece of the puzzle when it is time for advocates to come speak on your behalf should your position or the library program be threatened. Public librarians who have collaborated with you on projects are often happy to speak before the school board and may be excellent spokespeople. They will point out the ways that you have connected students and teachers to resources that benefit the district, and they are free!

Getting Administrative Support on Campus

You may have to provide information to your principal if, like in many cases, they have never been exposed to a school librarian that is capable, willing, and ready to collaborate with teachers.

One resource available free from AASL is a two-sided, three-fold brochure you can give your administrator to start a conversation about what you have to offer to the staff: http://www.ala.org/ala/mgrps/divs/aasl/aasl pubsandjournals/aaslbooksandprod/principalsmanual.pdf.

What are the top priorities for your principal?

- Is there a lot riding on high-stakes tests?
- Is the school focused on a specific subgroup that is in danger of slipping below the target score and putting the school into program-improvement status?
- Is the budget unmanageable? Will difficult cuts need to be made?
- Are parent groups high maintenance?
- Has the school gotten a bad reputation? Are students transferring out due to perceived problems?

Until you know what the principal will value, it is hard to promote yourself as a collaborative partner. When you know the goals and objectives of your administrator, you can position yourself as a resource and an advocate on the campus. Your activities in support of making the administrator's life easier will pay off dividends when you need the backing of the principal to pursue collaborative teaching opportunities.

Building Relationships on Campus

"Effecting change in any organization is a challenge. Change requires time and commitment—and a truckload of patience—but it is not possible without building a culture of trust." ~ Toni Buzzeo[1]

The school librarian must first develop relationships throughout the learning community. These don't necessarily have to be friendships, but before a collaborative effort can thrive, your future partners must know what you are able to offer. One factor to consider is how easy it is for teachers to approach you. If you're incredibly busy and the library is full or the schedule is packed, teachers may not want to ask you to do anything for them. Teachers may be wary of adding to your workload, especially if you seem to be overwhelmed.

Some school librarians naturally connect with classroom teachers seemingly without trying, while others find themselves in a closed environment that is very hard to break through. The key is to identify an approach that fits your personality. In some cases, a formal approach of scheduling meetings, structured partnerships, and joint planning is effective. In other cases, school librarians are more successful through informal friendships formed in teacher lounges, before faculty meetings, and in the hallways. The key is being receptive and proactive in making connections of all kinds.

Likely Candidates

New school librarians, or those who have recently transferred to a new environment, may not know where to start. Which teachers will be open and excited about collaboration, and which will be dismissive and demeaning?

- New teachers
  First-year teachers have not settled into a routine. They may be struggling with classroom management and look forward to working in an environment where the teacher-student ratio can be cut in half. If you have successful collaborations, you'll have a partner for years.
- Student teachers/master teachers
  Student teachers should have a collaborative experience, and master teachers usually recognize this. During that beginning period of time on campus, schedule a time for the student teachers to come for a tour to get oriented to the library and library services. These future teachers are often struggling with their placement and very appreciative when you offer them the resources they need.
- Teachers with huge classes
  Explore the half-class "station teaching" if teachers are experiencing classroom crowding. This model of instruction allows both teachers to divide the content, and each takes responsibility for planning and teaching part of it. Although you won't be able to co-teach, you can still work closely to give students a chance to take what they learn in the classroom and expand upon it by experimenting and exploring in the library. Stations are set up so that students can complete tasks independently, in pairs, or in small groups. This requires a lot of extra planning because everything has to be prepared and ready for students before visits can begin.
- Teachers involved in national board certification or teacher of the year
  Collaboration is often a requirement for national board certification and looks great on the application for teacher of the year. An advantage to working with this group of teachers is that you will be working with the best of the best.

- Teachers turned on to technology
  If your teachers have very few computers in the classroom, and you have more in the library, you can make a friend by offering to collaborate on cutting-edge technical projects.
- Your teacher buddies
  What does it say if you don't reach out to the very people that you enjoy the most? Are you worried that it will affect your friendship or that they will feel coerced into doing a project? If you are a strong school librarian, they will immediately realize that this relationship is beneficial for themselves and their students.
- Reluctant teachers
  Don't forget those Doubting Thomas types who have never collaborated before because a success with them can bring the rest of the teachers on board.

Paraprofessionals

To discuss collaboration and the paraprofessional, let's examine some definitions of library-classroom teacher collaboration.

> "Collaboration is the process of *shared creation*: two or more individuals with complementary skills interacting to create a shared understanding that none had previously possessed or could have come to on their own. Collaboration creates a shared meaning about a process, a product, or an event." ~ Michael Schrage[2]

> "Two or more equal partners who set out to create a unit of study based on content standards in one or more content areas plus information literacy standards, a unit that will be team-designed, team-taught, and team-evaluated." ~ Toni Buzzeo[3]

The reality that exists in many of our schools, especially elementary schools, is that not every school has a full-time teacher-librarian. The conditions required in the definitions above for collaboration to flourish are not present. True collaboration requires that both partners are equals, but we know that paraprofessionals do not have the same qualifications or status as credentialed teachers.

The school librarian can provide the resources for teachers and have them in the hands of the paraprofessional when the class arrives in the library. School librarians help paraprofessionals carry out their role of checking out materials when the initial collaboration with the teacher means the curriculum has been interpreted and the unit has been planned with teachers. In this way, the library continues to be used appropriately for instruction.

Collaborative Models

Dickinson (2006) describes a continuum of library-to-classroom teacher involvement starting with the lowest level of interaction and continuing through a truly integrated experience.[4]

Isolation.......... Cooperation......... Coordination.......... Collaboration

---

Recipe for Collaboration

Ingredients:
Collegiality
Knowledge
Respect
Trust

1. Bring all the ingredients to your meeting and engage in shared thinking about what you both want students to learn and be able to do.
2. Meet to do shared planning of activities or projects that will ensure that the students will learn.
3. Create a time line and divide responsibilities or create the instructional activities together.
4. Administer a pretest to see what the students already know, and review the results together to see if adjustments need to be made to assignments and learning activities.
5. Deliver instruction, coach students, and give them time to work.
6. Assess student work product together.
7. Share the results with others.

Of course, collaboration is not as easy as using the simple recipe above. The ingredients are complex; it takes time to develop collegiality, earn respect, and build trust. If you've never seen it in action, how do you know that your planning is *shared planning*?

You will have to examine your assumptions about how model collaborations should look. Many times, teachers will not understand that you are not simply offering to help teach what they want taught, but have different goals in mind as well. On the flip side, you should be clear about setting boundaries when teachers ask for more than you can do. You should have answers ready to the following questions before you begin the planning process with teacher(s).

1. Location
   • Are you willing to make trips to the classroom, or do you demand that the students come to you?
   • Is the library accessible at other times so that groups can continue working beyond the allotted instructional time?
   • Can students and teachers access the library portal from the classroom or home, or is the library the only place they can use the tools they need?
2. Time
   • How much time are you willing or able to set aside toward this collaboration?
   • Is there enough time for students to complete the project/lessons/activities, or will they start something that they can't finish properly?

3. Your informational-literacy goals
   • Will students be locating and evaluating information sources?
   • Will students learn how to extract and record relevant information?
   • Is there a component to help students understand and organize information?
   • Will you be helping students while they are synthesizing and communicating information?
   • Will you be addressing plagiarism concerns and helping them to cite sources correctly?

4. Your role
   • Do you want to be involved from start to finish, or simply with the "library part"?
   • Will you be helping students or groups to define the problem/question/topic, or will they come with an assignment where that is already set for them?
   • Will you spend time helping students narrow or broaden their topic once they dig in and start sorting their information?
   • Will you be helping students to plan their research process, or will it be set for them, or is that the whole point of the collaboration?
   • Will you be helping to assess the final product? Do you have time to attend group presentations if that is the format chosen? Do you have time to read research papers, and can you do it in a timely way?
   • Will you lead students through a self-assessment about their research experience?

Listed here are four common models of working relationships between teachers and school librarians often used to describe collaborative efforts. These models evolve from Loertscher's *Taxonomy of School Library Media Programs.*[5]

Model A: Cooperation

Just as the term implies, this model describes the school librarian and the teacher arranging their schedules so that they achieve mutually beneficial results. This often consists of teachers sending the class to the library in order to have preparation time. The school librarian is responsible for any activities that occur: story time, book talks, checking out books, silent sustained reading, information literacy or technology lessons, and the like. Even if the teacher is in attendance, the librarian is the one planning and directing the activities. Teachers may be physically present to help manage student behavior, but are engaged in grading papers, making copies, checking their e-mail, or pulling individual students for testing or intervention.

Model B: Coordination and Partnerships

This model involves the teacher and school librarians working together toward similar goals. Cooperation and partnerships require more commitment than coordination. This might mean working together on a grant to get money for resources (that will be housed and owned by the library) specific to a teacher's pet project. This is not limited to a single teacher, however; an administrator could initiate one for a school-wide project. It is not unusual to see specific grade levels, clubs, or teams working with the school librarian to set aside time, space, or materials in the library. Partnerships, by definition, also mean that both people involved are doing something. For example, the school librarian and a classroom teacher might be co-advisors of the associated student council. The council meetings might be held in the library, and both advisors may attend or alternate meetings.

This frequently occurs when a teacher assigns a project and sends the students to the library to work on it. The school librarian usually has advance notice of the assignment and may prepare by bookmarking electronic resources or pulling print materials. Increasingly, teachers will realize that the school librarian has specialized knowledge that can be shared with the students. For example, a teacher might be starting a genre study and will ask to bring the class for a lesson. The librarian may give a talk about the features of a genre, read several excerpts as teasers, and then give students time to browse and check out books of that genre to read. The teacher may then assign a book report, but the librarian wouldn't necessarily be involved from that point forward.

Model C: Integrated Instruction

This model of collaboration is more intensive than either coordination or cooperation. The school librarian and the teacher have a common objective and integrate classroom curriculum and library curriculum. This means they plan, implement, and evaluate together to create meaningful learning experiences that neither could duplicate alone.

Integrated instruction connects projects across traditionally separated subjects. Generally, students are given a real world problem that they need to study to formulate a solution. For example, students can examine problems such as drought in a project examining precipitation levels in different regions of a state and water usage patterns of residents. This will require math, social studies, and technology. Students will need to gather real-world data and maybe even talk to specialists in the field. Teachers create lessons in response to the barriers the students encounter in making sense of their data and applying it to the problem. The school librarian is intimately acquainted with the project and can guide students to the best resources available. Students and teachers, in consultation with the school librarian, flow freely between the classroom and the library as needed for the students to complete the project. The use of resources is authentic and unprogrammed, so you would not be expected to create or hunt down boring worksheets for students. Additionally, testable skills such as using an index, reading encyclopedia articles, and keeping track of references in order to cite them properly occur naturally.

Model D: Integrated Curriculum

This is similar to model C, except that it occurs across the school campus, in every classroom with every subject. The principal is instrumental because there must be extensive library staffing and resources to support library integration to this extent. The librarian(s) are truly the learning leaders as they continually master the content through co-teaching. In this model, the school librarian is equal to the teachers and is capable of developing and implementing curricula, as well as being an expert in twenty-first-century skills.

The Shared Planning Process

When school librarians and classroom teachers work together, they often start by looking at what they expect students to *know* and be able to *demonstrate* at the completion of the project or experience. The librarian will view this through the lens of information literacy, or what students need to know about accessing, evaluating, interpreting, and applying information. The teacher will often reference the state, national, or district content standards to be sure that the student will be able to perform on standardized tests. If the teacher does not see value in students mastering content while learning the research process, the collaboration will never get off the ground. You can find collaboration-planning sheets online or create your own; they can be extensive or simple depending on your style and that of the involved teacher(s).

The next issue is planning the direct instruction.

- Who will teach each part?
- How will the sequence of activities build upon each other?
- Where is the best place for each piece to be learned?

For most students to be successful, lessons should be sequenced so that they can learn and discover content easily in a guided experience or by inquiry. Instruction of specific skills, such as using subscription databases, should occur right when students need to complete assigned research tasks. Learning skills just in time to actually use them is the best way to make them meaningful and memorable. This instruction can be done whole group, in small groups, or by an automated tutorial that students can access independently. The more often students are given opportunities to practice using these skills, the more likely they will master not only that specific skill, but the more likely they are to return to that source in the future.

Assessment

What the Students Learned

Assessing learning is an important factor, both for the students involved and for rating the effectiveness of the collaboration. It is important to use a pretest to determine if students are ready to learn or *already know* what they are expected to learn. It may be necessary to provide background information or preview important skills for specific groups, like English learners. If students already know the content, the project should be adjusted so that it requires them to learn more deeply or apply what they already know to solve problems. Teachers and school librarians may also need to meet several times during the project; this is a good way to proceed because the students' progress (or lack thereof) may necessitate a change in plans. When the students' end product is assessed, both the teacher and the school librarian need to be a part of the grading. Students will quickly catch on if there will be no grade value assigned for what they are learning in the library. They should know up front that the school librarian will determine part of the grade.

What the Teacher Learned

When assessing the collaboration, the participating teacher should give you an honest evaluation of how the unit went from his or her perspective. This can be done in a variety of ways: you can create an online assessment form that the teacher(s) can complete when they have time, or you can have a pen-and-paper exit slip that you have them fill out, or with an interview where you jot down their feedback. Trying to get honest feedback can be quite difficult, especially if your collaborative partners are also friends who don't want to hurt your feelings. If you collaborate with several partners, you could allow them to respond anonymously so that it removes the temptation for others to give you a less-than-forthright review.

- What student learning was derived specifically from the expertise of the school librarian?
- Could you (the classroom teacher) have done as well, or better, on your own?
- How could the school librarian have been more effective?
- Was there wasted time?
- Were any of the activities "busy work," or were they germane to the project?
- What would you (the classroom teacher) change about the experience?
- Would you (the classroom teacher) be willing to collaborate (either using the same or a different unit) in the future?

The results of the teacher's assessment of the collaboration are important and can guide you in making progress toward instructional units that make a difference for students.

What You Learned

Part of becoming an accomplished teacher is reflecting on your teaching experiences on a regular basis. Ask yourself the same questions listed above to see if it was worth your time. Then look at the questions below to focus on student learning and how it was affected by your participation. This reflection may lead you to begin taking action specific to your expertise and practice.

- Were you able to supply a missing component that the classroom teacher would not have been able to provide on his or her own or in the classroom?

- Did students learn the information-literacy standards and were there any that remained unsuccessful even with your support? What would you do differently for these students if you were given another chance?
- Have you taught your teachers everything that you know? Are you out of new ideas? If you've exhausted your repertoire, is it time to learn something more?
- Did the teacher (or students) introduce you to new ideas, technologies, or strategies that you think might be successful as tools in the library in the future?
- Did you keep work samples of successful projects? Does the work product really highlight what the students learned and were able to do *because of their library experience*?

You have been actively assessing your collaborative activities, their challenges, possible solutions, and possible outcomes. In the next chapter, you will be given suggestions for judging the impact of your program.

Notes

1. Buzzeo, T. "Teaming up with Teachers May Be Difficult—But It's Not Impossible." *School Library Journal* (September 1, 2002), http://www.schoollibrary-journal.com/article/CA240062.html. Accessed November 24, 2009.

2. Schrage, M. *Shared Minds*. New York: Random House, 1990.

3. Buzzeo, T. *Collaborating to Meet Standards: Teacher/Library Media Specialist Partnerships for K–6*. Worthington, OH: Linworth, 2002.

4. Dickinson, G. K. "When Does Collaboration Start?" *School Library Media Activities Monthly* 23 (2): 56–58.

5. Loertscher, D. *Taxonomies of the School Library Media Program*. Englewood, CO: Libraries Unlimited, 1988.

CHAPTER 6

The ImpACTive Librarian

School librarians can share the research showing the impact of school librarians and well-stocked school libraries on the achievement of students. They will find that some if not many in the audience will suggest that this research has been done elsewhere. The best research to convince your colleagues of the importance of your library and your services in their lives will be the impact research you gather in your school.

Ten "ImpACT" Action Items for Every School Librarian

Do:

✓ Find out what the stakeholders think is important in a library program and then deliver it
✓ Keep track of numbers—count everything!
✓ Loosen policies—allow students to check out more items, give them access to more resources, and freedom to use the tools they prefer
✓ Conduct an action research project and submit results to collaborative efforts of school librarians to show that library programs positively impact student achievement.
✓ Keep up on professional reading to find out what is working elsewhere, what worked in the past, and what is being attempted—then try the best ones in your library.
✓ Analyze results from high-stakes tests to see if you can isolate areas where you or the library program is responsible
✓ Visit other school librarians that are experiencing success and learn what they are doing
✓ Link your program to other important activities or initiatives on campus
✓ Build your collection to fill curricular gaps, measure use of these materials, and compare student stores before and after your efforts

✓ Compare increases/decreases in reading scores to library factors: circulation of pleasure reading materials, reading incentive programs, book clubs, and find possible causal relationships

Our definitions:

impact

1. A forceful consequence of the school library program on student achievement and engagement. *The book had an impact on my thinking.*
2. The force exerted by the school librarian in introducing a new idea, concept, technology, or ideology. *The impact of the Internet and ubiquitous access to information.*
3. To have effect on, influence, or alter. *The library program has a positive impact on student achievement.*

Two-Part Quiz: Do You Know Your Stakeholders?

Part 1: Think about each group of stakeholders and make an educated guess as to how they would rank each of the areas.

Rank the most important as 10 and the least important as 1

Leave the (_____) section empty.

1. What is important to your students?
   _____ Getting good (or better) grades (_____)
   _____ Being accepted into (the right) college or being ready for a job (_____)
   _____ Access to computers and learning about new technology (_____)
   _____ Pursuing personal interests and pleasure reading (_____)
   _____ Having time in the library to read or study (_____)
   _____ Having a safe place to go (_____)
   _____ Managing activities and involvements (_____)
   _____ Help with homework and research projects (_____)
   _____ Having freedom to read books of own choosing (_____)
   _____ Choice in learning content that is interesting and important at own pace (_____)

2. What is important to the parents?
   _____ Student safety (_____)
   _____ Knowing assignments (_____)
   _____ Helping students with homework (_____)
   _____ Students being well-prepared for college or work (_____)
   _____ Keeping child out of trouble (_____)
   _____ Good grades (_____)
   _____ Students doing well on tests (_____)
   _____ Student wellness/happiness (_____)
   _____ Students getting appropriate support for learning English, special education, and/or the gifted and talented program (_____)
   _____ Opportunities to contribute by working in classroom or parent involvement (_____)

3. What is important to teachers?
   _____ Time (_____)
   _____ High-stakes tests (_____)
   _____ Discouraging and discovering plagiarism/cheating (_____)
   _____ Need to differentiate (_____)
   _____ Overcrowded classes (_____)
   _____ Parent concerns (_____)
   _____ Teaching difficult content (_____)
   _____ Learning new technology (_____)
   _____ Inspiring students to achieve (_____)
   _____ Students learning critical-thinking skills (_____)

4. What is important to your administrator?
   _____ High-stake test scores (_____)
   _____ Getting out (or staying out) of Program Improvement/NCLB (_____)
   _____ Student success (_____)
   _____ Staying within budget (_____)
   _____ Parents happy (_____)
   _____ Teachers happy (_____)
   _____ School reputation (_____)
   _____ Managing student behavior (_____)
   _____ Addressing struggling student needs and subgroup challenges (_____)
   _____ Pleasing district administrators (_____)

Part 2: Use the survey sheets to poll your stakeholders. Be sure to collect a large enough sample to make it meaningful. Ask a representative group of students, parents, and teachers (as well as your administrator) to tell you what is important to them. Compare the results by averaging the answers. Then write in the totals on the (_____).

Student Survey

Read each statement and rank them from 1 to 10, with 1 being most important to you and 10 being the least important.

_____ I want to get good grades.
_____ I want to be ready to go to college or get a good job.
_____ I want to use the computers and learn new things.
_____ I want to spend my time participating in sports or hobbies.
_____ I want a comfortable place to read or study.
_____ I want a safe place to go.
_____ I want help managing my time and staying organized with my schedule.
_____ I want help with homework and research projects.
_____ I want the freedom to read books that I find interesting.
_____ I want to choose to learn things that are interesting and important to me at my own pace.

Parent Survey

Read each statement and rank them from 1 to 10, with 1 being most important to you and 10 being the least important.

_____ I want my child to be safe at school.
_____ I want to know how my child is doing and about big assignments.
_____ I want my child to be able to get help with homework and projects.
_____ I want my child to be well prepared for college or work.
_____ I want to find activities that will keep my child out of trouble.
_____ I want my child to get good grades and do well on tests.
_____ I want my child to stay in school and learn to control negative behaviors.
_____ I want my child to be healthy and happy.
_____ I want my child to get support for learning English, special education, or the gifted and talented program.
_____ I want opportunities to contribute by working in the classroom or getting involved at the school.

Teacher Survey

Read each statement and rank them from 1 to 10, with 1 being most important to you and 10 being the least important.

_____ I need more time to get everything done.
_____ I worry that my students will not be ready for high-stakes testing.
_____ I struggle with students who practice plagiarism and cheating.
_____ I'm unable to address the needs for all the different levels in my classroom.
_____ My classes are overcrowded.
_____ Parents are a major source of stress.
_____ I spend a lot of time searching for resources when teaching difficult content.
_____ I need help using the required technology and staying current with new applications.
_____ I'm looking for ways to motivate my students.
_____ My students are lacking skills they will need to compete in the twenty-first century.

Administrator Survey

Read each statement and rank them from 1 to 10, with 1 being most important to you and 10 being the least important.

_____ I'm focused on our school achieving high test scores.

_____ I'm concerned about getting out (or staying out) of program-improvement status.

_____ I want all the students to succeed.

_____ My budget is out of balance and I have to make tough decisions.

_____ I spend a disproportionate amount of time dealing with parent concerns.

_____ My teachers are not performing to my satisfaction.

_____ The school's reputation is poor and interdistrict transfers are high.

_____ Poor student behavior is keeping achievement levels low.

_____ The school needs to focus on the needs of struggling students and subgroups.

_____ The district administrators have a direction that is difficult for me to implement.

Scoring: How well did you know your stakeholders? Which results surprised you? List at least two items from each question where the library is a part or all of the solution:

Students
-
-

Parents
-
-

Teachers
-
-

Administrators
-
-

School Librarians! Light that Fire!

One popular magazine for elementary school librarians is called *Library-*

Sparks.[1] This is a good descriptor for school librarians who offer the spark for learning, and, contrary to popular belief, this is not just with books. School libraries increasingly have offered a variety of media types from the time when audiovisual resources moved into the library in the 1960s. This has moved at the present time into including electronic and technological gadgets. School librarians have the requisite technical know-how necessary to succeed in the digital age and can share their knowledge and skills with their teachers and students. This spark can inspire students and teachers to consider their library something reflecting the "more" that they learn exists there:

- Cybrary
- Learning commons
- Learning lab
- Libratory
- Media center
- Information center
- Innovation station
- The resource place
- Synergy center
- T and I club (technology and information)

School libraries provide the atmosphere and tools for connection, comprehension, and engagement, the hooks that students need in this day and age in order to learn well. As you are reading this book, you should be considering the anecdotal evidence that supports the view that the library is more than a book warehouse because there are situations that illustrate this value occurring in school libraries every day. You need to take the time to enter these instances into a *reflective journal* so they can be remembered rather than lost over time.

We have solid evidence that there is a relationship between effective school libraries and student test scores from the extensive statewide studies of Keith Curry Lance and the Colorado State Library research team. Know what the evidence overwhelmingly shows, and be ready to speak about it. Study the research foundation paper published and updated regularly by Scholastic, *School Libraries Work!* You can download a free copy at http://www2.scholastic.com/content/collateral_resources/pdf/s/slw3_2008.pdf.

One might ask: Who knows best what should be happening in your school library, and how do you share that information? The school librarian is the expert in managing the school library, but these activities are seldom understood by those in the school. All the effort spent in being a good manager is worthless if the needs of the stakeholders aren't being met. The *perception* of the school library is more powerful than the technical quality of the catalog records, the condition of the books, or the neatness of the shelves. In fact, neat shelves and books in good condition may indicate that the library is little used. The school librarian should collect measures to show how well the needs of the stakeholders are being met. Some traditional measurements are shown below.

Traditional Measurements

Many ways are used to report figures that serve as evidence of library activities that *may* impact student learning. These measurements are quantitative in nature and are key factors found time and again in high-performing schools:

- Collection statistics
  - Number of books per student
  - Average age of materials
  - Variety of formats
  - Monetary value of materials
  - Collection map showing adequate coverage of core content areas

- Library staffing levels
  - Hours open
  - Credentialed staff
  - Paraprofessionals
  - Volunteers
  - Student workers

- Circulation/library usage statistics
  - Number of materials checked out (by category)
  - Number of patron or class visits
  - Number of reference questions answered
  - Hours of in-library computer usage
  - Number of hits on library portal
  - Subscription databases and electronic resource usage
  - Number of items reserved or requested offsite through the online catalog
  - Interlibrary loans

- Collaboration between the librarian and teacher
  - Number of meetings
  - Activities/lessons in library
  - Information literacy or technology standards taught
  - Results

- Librarian's role as learning leader
  - Professional development attended by librarian
  - Professional development opportunities that the librarian provides (and number of participants)

All of the statistics listed above are indicators of things that you do or that the library program provides that directly or indirectly support student achievement. Showing a positive change that is attributable to your work is a good way to showcase your efforts.

It may seem like you are counting everything that you do, and that is good! Reporting what is happening in the school library is an important part of advocacy. While there are many things that school librarians do in the management of the program that aren't particularly impressive to the layperson, don't forget to report on these tasks. They are often the very things that only you are able to do. Examples of this include ordering and processing new books, mending materials, shifting the collection, correcting bibliographic records, weeding, sending out overdue notices, and the like. However, these can't be the only things you do. If a principal has to make budget cuts and thinks that all you do is circulate and shelve books, you may find your position reduced or eliminated.

If these management tasks are how you are spending *all* your time, you may want to examine what effect you really have on student achievement. Managing a library requires a balance between doing library administrative tasks and actively working with patrons. Your teachers and students and their needs come first when a choice must be made.

What We Aren't Measuring

Even with a concerted effort to report on everything that is happening in the library, there are always many things we don't capture. The examples that follow are just a few ideas for you to think about. Notice that the big question simply leads to further questions. It will be your job to answer these questions by searching for or creating assessments or ways of measuring that make sense.

Question: *How well have students mastered information-literacy skills?*

- It is hard to believe how often we do not know this except anecdotally. Do we have an agreed-upon common assessment tool using state library standards or AASL's Standards for the 21st-Century Learner?[2]
  - Can students find information?
  - Can students evaluate the information they find?
  - Can students apply what they find to the project they are working on or question they are trying to answer?
  - Can students communicate the information they find ethically and using consistent formatting?

Question: *Does the librarian inspire a love of reading and literature?*

- Do students participate in reading incentive programs of their own volition or is it a requirement? Do they sustain their interest or get burned out after a few years? Are they reading for prizes or reading for pleasure?
- Do students pick books based solely on "how many points" can be earned or by reading level even if they are not particularly interested in the contents?
- Are there waiting lists for popular books? Do "non-incentive" books, even new and attractive ones, gather dust?

- Do adults on campus model the same love of reading that we hope to inspire in students? Is there a teacher/parent book club?
- Do students express a love for reading? Is there evidence of students actively engaged in reading, or is the library more a computer and activity center?

Question: *How strong is the linkage with the public library, and is there any way to connect that with student academic improvement?*

- How do we connect with public librarians to find out if our students are chronic users of the public libraries?
- Are school library/public library collaborations in part responsible for increased use of the public library?
- Are students more likely to visit during the school year during the hours and/or days when the school library is closed or when school is not in session (summer, winter, or spring breaks)?
- Are students introduced to the summer reading program through the school library or do they discover it independently?
- How much does involvement with the summer reading program prevent summer learning loss?

Question: *How much of the student computer usage is for fun or entertainment versus academic endeavors?*

- Is there any merit to having links to fun sites from your library portal?
- How do we deal with privacy concerns? Is it any of our business what students do on the computer?
- How do we differentiate between what is a game that reinforces skills as opposed to a game with no value?
- Why do we approve of reading books for pleasure, but discourage reading online information for pleasure?
- Are students practicing Internet safety while using the library computers? Do they know the common ways they can be scammed or tricked into giving out personal information?

Question: *How is the library embracing new formats and technology?*

- Are e-books becoming a regular part of your library collection?
- Do you check out laptops, iPods, e-readers, or other devices?
- What student-owned devices are allowed in the library to access information? Can students access free and open Wi-Fi? Are cell phones banned?
- Are students using the in-library computers to read e-books? Does this cause long waits for other students?

Question: *Are the students ready for jobs when they graduate?*

- Are students helped to find part-time jobs while they are still in high school?
- Do you help them learn the skills needed for the different occupations?

Question: *Are students encouraged to become lifelong learners?*

- Are students introduced to the resources available in libraries in the area?
- Are students taught how to find information in all types of libraries?
- How do you work with other teachers to help students learn about the recreational and cultural experiences they should enjoy as adults?

Question: *Are students ready for college?*

Ultimately, school librarians want students to have the skills they need to be successful should they pursue a higher education. It might be hard to see this as a goal you are working toward with your kindergarten students! Still, vertical articulation of skills needed for success at the next level is important. It sets the foundation for why expenditures for quality school libraries staffed by credentialed librarians are absolutely essential beginning with the lowest grades.

We have only to look at what college professors and librarians say about incoming freshmen to know that we must start earlier to build information-literate students:

> College librarians are also in a unique position to assess new students' college readiness. It doesn't matter whether they work in an elite liberal arts institution, a community college, or a major research university—librarians also observe students' lack of the knowledge and skills they need to succeed, in particular their lack of information-retrieval and information-evaluation skills.[3]

Brainstorm three additional questions worthy of investigation:

1.
2.
3.

Action Research and the School Library

Teachers are searching for easier ways to tackle the everyday, real-world problems they are experiencing in their classrooms. Teacher accountability for student-achievement results should not start and end with the classroom teacher. The school librarian and other support staff have responsibility for the achievement of students. Action research is an important way that we can measure the impact of the library program, and these results can provide the "aha!" to decision-makers as to the importance of maintaining and investing in school libraries.

Action research measures evidence of the qualities found in the many different aspects of student learning in the school library. It requires reflection and discussion on the part of the school librarian and the participating teachers, and this is based on the needs and progress of students. It is a chance to try out innovative ways of instruction, embedding the library component into a project, or implementing an inquiry-based unit. Administrators are searching for documentation of evidence-based practice that leads to academic achievement. Action research is one way to demonstrate your impact.

"Rather than dealing with the theoretical, action research allows practitioners to address those concerns that are closest to them, ones over which they can exhibit some influence and make change." ~ Eileen Ferrance.[4] Ferrance continues:

> Action research is not about doing research on or about people, or finding all available information on a topic looking for the correct answers. It involves people working to improve their skills, techniques, and strategies. Action research is not about learning why we do certain things, but rather how we can do things better. It is about how we can change our instruction to impact students.

The action research process has many different models, but generally follows some standard steps.[5]

1. Identify a problem.
   Clearly define a specific problem. Beware of the problems where the library has little if any impact. Your time and resources are limited, and you can't solve problems unrelated to the library without sacrificing the opportunity to focus on the problems that exist. The strategy of improving the quality of services in the school library involves prioritizing the importance of problems that teachers encounter with students. You will need to get the input of your teachers so that you can focus on the problems that you all agree are important. Four problems worthy of further study are:
   • Plagiarism is rampant.
   • Students can't find information.
   • Reading scores are plummeting—students indicate that reading is boring.
   • Students are surfing aimlessly on the Internet.

2. Collect baseline data.
   It is important to measure student performance before making any changes. If you do not measure how students are doing first, then there will be no way to evaluate whether a change makes a difference. This initial gathering of data provides a comparison point to help assess whether a change you make is having the intended effect.
   • Teachers report on the cases of plagiarism or suspected cheating.
   • Put a yes/no T-chart on the library exit door with a pen on a string. Have the question "Did you find what you needed?" in big letters at the top.
   • Survey students about their reading habits and what they want to read.
   • Have one or two classes use the library computers to complete a research task. Keep track of how long students take on the computers in relation to the number of reliable sources they are able to document.

3. Review literature and brainstorm solutions.
   - Check in library and teacher journals.
   - Meet with teachers and include their ideas.

   Steps 4–6 are the "transformation steps."

4. Develop a program of action based on data
   - Provide lessons and activities to address the problems.
   - Set up a research buddy program so that students can work in pairs, especially if you can team up high- and low-performing students.
   - Purchase an appropriate database (or just use a trial version as a test) and provide training to students and teachers.
   - Coordinate genre talks with classes to get students exposed to a wide variety of pleasure reading possibilities—maybe they just haven't been turned on to romance, sci-fi, or mystery.

5. Collect, review, and interpret data generated.
   - Collect data about the results by asking teachers to count instances, release scores, or survey respondents for change in behavior or attitude.
   - Were incidents of plagiarism decreased?
   - Were students more successful at finding information?
   - Was student research time maximized—did they find usable information more quickly?

6. Reflection and sharing.
   - What worked and what didn't?
   - What could still be tried?
   - Which processes will be standardized and put into place long-term?

Steps 4 through 6 of this process are iterative, and the entire process should be repeated to find and solve additional problems.

Equity

Even within the same school district, there are often large discrepancies in staffing, collections, and services in the libraries. Schools serving low socio-economic groups also tend to have fewer volunteers, donations, and sources of funding for the library. Many other factors have major influences on achievement: teacher quality, academic rigor of curriculum, economically disadvantaged families, learning disabilities, and limited English proficiency. In some ways, the demographics of the school seem to drive the test scores; but we know from the evidence in *School Libraries Work!* that investing in quality school libraries makes a difference, even controlling for those other factors. In closing the achievement gap and creating educational equity, school boards, superintendents, and principals need to know that school libraries are a logical first place to start.

Making the case in your district:

- Does the library budget as a school line item account for a difference in reading scores? Try plotting the two sets of data in a line graph.
- Do the schools with the highest proficiency in student reading scores have credentialed librarians *and* paraprofessionals?
- Do high-performing schools have library media centers with longer open hours?
- Do students who score highest on reading tests attend schools with larger library collections and newer average copyright dates?
- Do any schools have "distinguished school" or other award status? If so, what is the level of staffing in the school library? How does this compare to other schools that have not obtained the same recognition?
- Are library worker's hours tied to the number of enrolled students? Do crowded high-need schools have the same number of open hours as smaller schools?
- Where is the money and collection growth coming from?
  - Who is actively searching for and writing grants for library acquisitions?
  - Does the PTA regularly fund the library?
  - Are a large number of quality donations received to supplement the collection?

Keep track of what you do and count everything. Share information about how the library impacts student achievement. Survey your patrons to see if your assumptions about what is important to them are correct. Consider new ways to measure your impact or initiate an action-research project. Finally, work for equity in your school library program. In the next chapter, help is provided in getting funding for the school library.

Notes

1. LibrarySparks is an upstart publication. Check http://www.highsmith.com/librarysparks/ for subscription information.

2. AASL's Standards for the 21st-Century Learner can be purchased or downloaded for free from http://www.ala.org/ala/mgrps/divs/aasl/guidelinesandstandards/learningstandards/standards.cfm.

3. Rettig, J. "Frame of Reference: School Libraries and the Educational Ecosystem." *Change: The Magazine of Higher Learning* 41 (2) (2009): 28–29.

4. Ferrance, E. *Action Research*. Providence, RI: Northeast and Islands Regional Educational Laboratory at Brown University, 2000.

5. Here is a brief bibliography if you want to learn more about action research: Johnson, A. P. *A Short Guide to Action Research*. Boston: Allyn and Bacon, 2007. Sykes, J. A. *Action Research: A Practical Guide for Transforming Your School Library.* Englewood, CO: Libraries Unlimited, 2002.

CHAPTER 7

The Librarian as BenefACTor

School libraries are often the first place to have budgets cut. No library can survive if no new resources are available for students. It takes a very short time for a collection to become stagnant and not useful to teachers and students. It becomes essential for the school librarian to do as much as possible to get money to supplement the limited funds budgeted for the school library.

In times when the economic condition of schools is desperate, others will be looking for help in funding their programs. Sometimes working together can be beneficial to all.

Ten "BenefACTor" Action Items for Every School Librarian

Do:

✓ Find local grants that you have a good chance of obtaining
✓ Solicit help from local service organizations
✓ Volunteer to help write funding proposals for others in your school and district and see if you can include a component for library materials
✓ Initiate an annual fund-raising event (such as a 5K race, a skating party, or a cow plop)
✓ Offer books for sale through book-club magazines (like Scholastic) and use the earned points to build your collection
✓ Hold a book fair and find a way to let parents and students purchase items from a teacher wish list
✓ Acknowledge contributions big and small when they occur, including a regular practice of recognizing students and staff
✓ Organize capital campaigns for major projects whether or not it involves the library
✓ Research the feasibility of starting a library endowment
✓ Coordinate philanthropic activities that benefit the community

Our definitions:

benefactor A person who helps other people or institutions (especially with financial help). *Many school libraries rely on benefactors to provide resources for teachers and students.*

"No Way to Fail" Quiz

Challenge your assumptions. All the answers can be right, and all can be wrong depending on your situation and when and how you proceed. Which answer(s) make you most comfortable when you are looking for library benefactors? Would you have a different approach when asking one person than another? What would make the difference in your approach, and what would you see as the difference in the response?

1. When you ask for money, the best thing to do is:
   a. Ask for more than you need because it is likely that you'll get less.
   b. Ask for exactly what you need, no reason to be greedy.
   c. Ask for less than you actually need because it is embarrassing to seem greedy and because the large numbers will scare them off from giving anything.

   Answer: Instead of focusing on the scarcity of money, time, or people, show that there is an abundance of desire to make the library better through leadership and pursuit of a vision. Ask for realistic amounts, but do not shy away from asking for large amounts. If you get partial funding, you can approach other organizations asking for a matching amount.

   Most potential donors like to know exactly how you will be spending the funds. For example, if you ask for money to provide additional resources for your students, does this mean you will buy books that will bear the donor's name on the nameplate, or are you going to pay for a database subscription and thus need the same amount of money to continue the subscription for another year? Some donors will be willing to purchase new things for the library if they know you have additional help from another source. The one thing you must always remember is that those paying taxes to support schools may consider that is as much of a "donation" as they are willing to give. When this happens, you need to thank them and consider a different approach.
2. The right time to ask for money is:
   a. When the library can't survive without it.
   b. When you have time to fill out all the paperwork.
   c. When you have an unexpected need that cannot be met with the present budget.
   d. When the library is thriving.

   Answer: Soliciting funds for the school library is an ongoing activity that has no right or wrong time. Whether the system is flush or desperate, there are always needs that cannot be met with the annual budget allocation. Finding time to write grants and approach organizations for funding is a continual challenge for working school librarians. However, if you find you suddenly have a new textbook adoption that will make your present collection of resources insufficient, you may need to try to find funds to support this. When the school library is thriving, the amount of time you assign to this need not be as great, and it may be time to "rest on your laurels."

3. If I receive money, the best thing to do is:
   a. Save it for something that is really needed later or when I have time to get an order prepared.
   b. Spend it right away, even if there isn't a great need, because it could be taken away.
   c. Share with other concerns in the school. Maybe they'll support the library later.

Answer: Instead of focusing on getting your fair share or protecting your piece of the pie, work with other groups to make the entire pie larger. When you help them with their proposal, they will help you with yours. They will also be willing to add resources for the library when they are asking for funding. For example, if you find a way to support the chess club, perhaps by providing space, purchasing chessboards or timers, and buying books to support learning the game, then they should remember you when they are applying for a larger grant and include you in the planning. It is also likely that resources that are a part of the grant would be happily housed in the library rather than one classroom.

4. In order to convince others to contribute to the library, I need to:
   a. Persuade everyone that the library is the neediest program on campus.
   b. Demonstrate that the library is the most worthy recipient.
   c. Engage others in ways they can help you to find money.

Answer: There are two schools of thought on this subject. One way of thinking is that sources of funds will understand that the school library is both worthy and needy, and therefore it is in your best interest not to compare your program to others on campus. This is especially true if you, in competing for funds, say things that may cause animosity in the future. On the other hand, when you passionately believe in the importance of what you are trying to do and cannot hope for success with no additional funding, you must point out inequities and show the ways that money going into the library facility and collection benefits all the students and all the teachers in the building.

5. I can measure the success of how money is raised and spent by:
   a. Outcomes such as test scores, number of participants, items borrowed, or collection size and currency.
   b. Impact that is made by asking for subjective data such as student or teacher satisfaction.
   c. Willingness of sponsors/grantors to give again when asked.

Answer: All of these methods are good measuring sticks to use when evaluating efforts at growing your fiscal influence. Using many different measures is advantageous because it allows you to answer future challenges. For example, if someone challenges circulation figures as a measure, you can follow up by showing them a patron-satisfaction survey that indicates that students responded that they were more likely to find what they were looking for.

6. The best way to approach prospective donors is to appeal to their:
   a. Civic duty
   b. Idealism

c. Emotions

d. Status in the community

Answer: All of these are ways to tap into good reasons for donating, and this may be influenced by a person's generation. Many seniors feel that there is a civic duty to donate time and money to worthy causes, while people born in the 1950s and 1960s are generally more idealistic. Young parents are emotionally invested in the success of their student's school and will want to participate because it is the right thing to do. Finally, wealthy benefactors are often looking for recognition when they give large amounts. They may like to have their name attached to a project, such as the O'Brien Library, the Franklin Family Library Nights, or the Wilson Homework Lab. It often doesn't cost anything more than a sign or plaque to give recognition to major donors.

Service organizations can be encouraged to make sizeable donations to honor one of their prominent members at his or her retirement. One very aggressive school librarian read the obituaries to find families that might want to make a donation to honor their relative who had attended the school. Your service organization might also be pleased to have a program showing new technologies used in school libraries. Take along students to help with the demonstration, and have your proposed purchases list ready.

7. When soliciting funds, it is important to:

a. Dream big: Be optimistic with well-reasoned arguments ready to back up your plans.

b. Play it smart: Be sensitive to the audience you are addressing so that the appeal seems personalized.

c. Know your stuff: Be technically perfect with detailed information that can answer all questions.

d. Stay grounded: Be sure to wait before acting prematurely by reminding others the project will occur only if it is funded.

e. Tell it like it is: Be ready to share stories and facts that support the need for funding.

f. Include as many as you can in the project.

Answer: Again, all of these are important factors when asking for funds. If you find that you have one area that is lacking, be honest that you will need help in that area. For example, if your proposal is highly technical and relies on understanding technology beyond your comfort level, point out how important this funding is to helping you obtain that specialized assistance. The more people you can serve with the funding you receive, the more likely you will receive funds. If you are asking for new technology that will be used by the entire school, it may have a better result than a request for more picture books for the kindergarten.

From First to Worst

Needless to say, finding sustaining funds for the library can be a daunting task, and without sufficient funding, even the most respected program can fail. How is it that strong school libraries can morph from vibrant programs to having their doors closed without the parents and teachers raising a fuss? It often happens so gradually that it goes relatively unnoticed.

Administrators view the library as a cost center because it doesn't generate any revenue for the school. School board members may have little if any knowledge that the library is an actual classroom, and they see it as a frill that the budget can't sustain. Some teachers fear their class sizes will become much larger if they keep these "special" activities, and other teachers fear they will lose their own classrooms if they fight for the librarian's position.

The demise of a school library program can be slow. One scenario follows:

An elementary school of 750 students has a library open from 7 a.m. to 5 p.m. every school day, staffed with one school librarian and two paraprofessionals. It is an exemplary library, and considered to be the heart of the school.

Year 1	One of the paraprofessionals retires and the principal decides not to hire a replacement.
Year 2	The school librarian is asked to take on additional duties, such as teaching one or two reading groups each day, but the library remains open under the supervision of the remaining paraprofessional.
Year 3	Cuts are made at other schools and the full-time paraprofessional is bumped to another school. The new paraprofessional files a grievance about not having a duty-free lunch. The library is closed at lunchtime for students.
Year 4	The school librarian is assigned to two or more schools and splits time between locations, but the paraprofessional is still keeping the door open.
Year 5	The paraprofessional position is reduced to six hours a day, and the school librarian is only able to spend one day a week at the school. The library is closed at lunch and before school.
Year 6	The paraprofessional is further reduced to four hours a day. The library is only open in the morning until lunch begins. The school librarian is assigned additional sites and is only available on a drop-in basis. The library is not given a book budget. No new resources are purchased.
Year 7	The school librarian position is eliminated.
Year 8	The paraprofessional is reduced to 3.75 hours a day and loses benefits. The library is open from 8:30 a.m. to 12:15 p.m. No new books or resources are added to the library shelves and the catalog, and what is left no is longer appealing enough for students to take to their rooms or home.
Year 9	The paraprofessional is given two schools to manage on 3.75 hours a day and rotates weeks between schools. The library is then open every other week from 8:30 a.m. to 12:15 p.m. The catalog has severe inaccuracies because inventory has not been done in many years, and the teachers have become accustomed to

taking things from the library without permission when the para-professional is not working.

Year 10   The library is closed because it has such limited access as to make it irrelevant, and it is no longer valued as a resource. Rebuilding the library's collection will be very costly and slow. Even with an influx of funding, it will not be easy to replace what has been lost. To purchase the best and only the best means a limited number of items can be selected each year, and one would not want to have multiple copies of books just to fill the shelves.

This scenario might seem far-fetched to some. In fact, the gradual erosion of library services by the decisions of principals, superintendents, and school board members is a familiar story in many places. Although there are many states that mandate that schools must have libraries, school librarians, and support staff, one only needs to look at California to see what happens when a measure is passed to severely cut funding to schools. The People's Initiative to Limit Property Taxation, Proposition 13, was an amendment to the California Constitution in 1978. California's excellent schools began their downward slide to the bottom of test scores across the United States in almost every area.

In any state, when the professional school librarian position is not man-dated or when mandates are suspended, school library programs are marginal-ized. Administrators trim their school budgets by reducing funding for materials, cutting the hours of service, and replacing certified school librarians with a teacher one period a day or assigning paraprofessionals or even recruit-ing volunteers. This trend, replacing school librarians with noncertified staff and replacing classified staff with unpaid workers, devalues library work and reduces the library's importance to that of a place to come to waste 30 minutes of time each week.

The downhill plunge after Proposition 13 continues to gain momentum. Economic downturns are affecting every state in the union, some more deeply than others, and once the bottom is reached, the climb back up the hill will be a very steep and very slow process.

Budget Cuts

The school library budget may be set as a line item by the principal, but administered by the school librarian. Notice that the budget above does not include the salaries and benefits of school library personnel. Those figures would be included in the larger school budget and paid for from district funds.

One reason that administrators and decision-makers use when justifying cuts to the school library program is literature saying that school libraries aren't needed when everyone has access to the Internet. Some suggest there is evidence of lessened library usage by teachers and students when educators must teach to the test and the textbook. Outside research is a time-consuming frill. Here are four stated reasons for this justification in cutting the library professionals and services:

- Students have Internet access at home and in class.
- Teachers have access to streaming video through YouTube and subscription services.
- High-stakes testing and adherence to the curriculum allows less time for students to visit the library or use class time for inquiry-learning projects.
- Student and teachers may be using the library portal in lieu of physical visits.

When a decision is made to cut the library, it may be the site library budget that is trimmed, or it could be that staffing will be affected. When cuts are mandated, the certified school librarian is a big target. This is usually the largest expense, especially as compared to the support-staff person. The library doors can stay open without a school librarian, and some principals think that teachers should pick up the slack by teaching information literacy in the classroom. Sometimes administrators believe that a certified or classified position can be cut temporarily until the budget recovers, but it is rare to ever have the position or hours reinstated, even when times are flush. Whether this is a case of "out of sight, out of mind," learning to live with less, or having no one left to ask as competing interests get preference, the truth is that once a cut is made, it is a death knoll for school libraries.

Many arguments and compelling reasons can be offered in support for keeping school librarians. Students (and sometimes teachers) may have an unhealthy respect for anything they see in print, ignoring the fact that just because it is in a newspaper or magazine or on the Internet does not mean that it is relevant, authoritative, or even true. Students cut and paste answers or information on a topic and turn this in as research, learning little in the process. When the professional school librarian goes away, teachers stop assigning true research projects because their students have limited access to the resources they need or the person with the expertise to teach students the research process. Since student achievement is measured by multiple-choice assessments and the occasional essay, real-life skills like reading, analyzing, and synthesizing data into written documents or presentations is no longer the focus of instruction. Teachers need help to realize that these skills contribute to success in high-stakes testing, and the certified school librarian is still the best person to tackle the teaching of this strand. Paraprofessionals do not have the expertise and teachers do not have the time to do it in their place.

When the district's school libraries' budgets or your building-level school library budget is threatened, suggest that the answer is not to cut programs or personnel, but to find creative ways to decrease program expenses or to find other ways to increase funds to support the library program. Not only will you be required to tell them, you must be prepared to show them concrete figures. This means you need to understand school district funding.

Understanding Funding

Private schools fund their libraries directly from tuition and donations. They are rarely eligible for government funding. However, most private school personnel are well trained and well experienced in fund-raising to support the school. Also, many students who attend private schools have families with income to support fund-raising activities.

When you work in a public school, your funding generally comes from one of the following five places:

1. State funds: This may be a line item that can be used only for school libraries or it may be part of a block grant that allows local decision-makers flexibility in how it is spent. Many times, it is based on a formula that gives a certain amount per pupil.
2. Federal funds: These are sometimes earmarked for special projects, programs, or populations. This includes title money, block grants, chapter grants, stimulus funds, and competitive grants. Often these are one-time monies that are allocated for specific purposes and must be spent within defined guidelines and require extensive reporting.
3. Local funds: In many locations, these come from property taxes or bonds and may account for a large percentage of some school budgets, although this is not true in California. Proposition 13 halted cities from raising property taxes to support schools. In other states, such as New Mexico, much of the funding comes from the state, and districts have budgets carefully scrutinized by the state's department of education personnel. Local funds are allocated by the local board of education, and the district may have chosen to have site-based management. In this case, funds go to the local school for distribution to programs. In other cases, districts develop a per-pupil allocation to schools based on the numbers of students enrolled. School library funding may also be based on a per-pupil allocation for library resources.
4. Private funds from parent-teacher organizations, educational foundations, companies seeking to be educational partners, service organizations, or other entities with grant dollars for projects addressing their concerns.
5. Fund-raising that happens primarily through sales, events, performances, providing services, donations, or games of chance and other activities that are usually school-wide efforts.

School librarians must learn how to find out what is allocated to school libraries. This is often a separate line item in the local school budget. Ask your school secretary to help you learn how to read the district budget because this is the one over which you may have a little control. It is usually a very complicated document, but it is open to the public's scrutiny.

Depending upon the kind of funding within the district, you will learn if you are given a per-pupil allocation at the district level to all schools, or it may be distributed from a central office for school libraries in the district. In either of these cases, you must negotiate any changes with the district administrators.

In some districts, funds are given to the principal, who may distribute them, or these funds may be distributed at the discretion of a site council. When it is the principal who allocates funds, you will need to address your needs to a single person. If the allocation for funds for the school is in the hands of the site council, you will need to plead your case to a committee. This is one of the reasons that school librarians are urged to work for election to the site council if the school budget is managed by this group.

When you decide that the only alternative is to try to raise funds to help support your library, you need to discuss your options with your teachers and your principal to enlist their suggestions, and in the case of the principal, enlist permission to undertake this approach. Fund-raising is discussed in more detail below.

Legislative Advocacy

Because public schools get most of their funding from governmental entities, formal advocacy must take place at all levels of government: local, state, and national. Larger school districts often have someone available in the state capital and even Washington, D.C., to help secure funding for education within their districts. Personnel in smaller districts must support the efforts of their teacher unions and depend upon their own efforts to tell their legislators about the needs for the education of students. These groups will be lobbying for general education and usually not for specific programs.

At the national level, the American Library Association has an office in Washington, D.C. to monitor congressional legislative efforts for all types of libraries including school libraries. This office sends legislative alerts to members to write or call their members of Congress with specific instructions about the bills under consideration. They also sponsor a legislative day in the spring and librarians from all over the U.S. arrive to visit their members of Congress to discuss libraries. Unfortunately it is difficult for most school librarians to be available on that particular day. However, they are able to make visits to their local congressional offices to present the status of school libraries.

Some statewide school library organizations have paid lobbyists who work at the state level, and most have legislative days set aside for organized visits made to the offices of elected officials while the body is in session. Many schedule formal days in the district for visits to the local office maintained by the elected official. Legislative advocacy is discussed in more depth in chapter 9.

While it may not seem that you can have much impact on funding for your school library through these efforts, they do ultimately affect individual schools. One of the reasons you need to keep your national and state legislators aware of your needs is that is the only way they will learn of how what they do affects how you help students in your school.

Grants

In 2001, the Improving Literacy through School Libraries program was authorized at $250 million, but actual funding has never been appropriated at that level. Sponsored by the U.S. Department of Education, this money allows certain low-income public schools to update library collections, expand Internet connections, buy new technology, provide professional development for library staff, and extend library hours. Local education agencies (LEAs) in which at least 20 percent of students served are from families with incomes below the poverty line may apply for these funds.[1] As this book goes into production, this earmarked funding is being threatened with moving back into general funding.

If your district qualifies to apply for these funds, you have a very good chance of receiving funds. Notice that the initial appropriation was increased in 2004 and has remained fairly stable for every year thereafter.[2]

2008
Appropriation: $19,144,597
Number of New Awards: 60
Average Awards: $250,000
Range of Awards: $30,000 to $500,000

2007
Appropriation: $19,486,170
Number of New Awards: 78
Average Awards: $190,000
Range of Awards: $30,000 to $300,000

2006
Appropriation: $19,486,170
Number of Awards: 78
Average Awards: $190,000
Range of Awards: $30,000 to $300,000

2005
Appropriation: $19,683,264
Number of Awards: 85
Average Awards: $225,000
Range of Awards: $26,000 to $350,000

2004
Appropriation: $19,842,236
Number of Awards: 92
Average Awards: $212,000
Range of Awards: $30,000 to $399,000

2003
Appropriation: $12,500,000
Number of Awards: 73
Average Award: $165,000
Range of Awards: $20,000 to 335,000

2002
Appropriation: $12,418,750
Number of Awards: 94
Average Award: $130,000
Range of Awards: $24,000 to $350,000

Other grants that school librarians should explore include:

Laura Bush Foundation for America's Libraries, http://www.laurabush foundation.org/

Partnership for a Nation of Learners Community Collaboration Grants

Institute of Museum and Library Services, http://www.imls.gov/applicants/ grants/communityCollaboration.shtm

Service Organizations

Practically every town of moderate size has groups of individuals that devote themselves to making the community a better place. Developing a relationship with these organizations can lead to donations, volunteers for projects and fund-raisers, and working together for common causes. Your local chamber of commerce should have a comprehensive list of service clubs, but the following organizations are likely to exist in your area:

- Benevolent and Protective Order of Elks
- Junior League
- Kiwanis
- Knights of Columbus
- Lion's Club
- Optimist Club
- Rotary
- Soroptimist Club

Regularly invite members of these clubs to participate in your events. Offer to have them use your library as a meeting location so they can get a quick tour. Whether it is a career day, a fund-raiser, or you ask them to come in and read to a class on Dr. Seuss' birthday, invitations to these local movers and shakers keeps your cause in their minds.

Fund-raising

School librarians, like most other teachers, give of their own time and money to create the best instructional environment possible. This includes purchasing special items like puppets, supplemental curriculum, bulletin board materials, or even books. Since school librarians are rarely independently wealthy, fund-raising is an important option for supplementing the budget. The task of putting together fund-raisers falls outside of the job of running the library. The school administrator has an expectation, though, that any major effort requires participation by all staff members. In turn, the funds raised have some benefit to the library. In a school, parent, caregivers, or retired persons from the community may be enlisted as volunteers in your library, to manage the volunteer program, and for any outside activities. Based on the success of public libraries developing "friends" groups, school libraries need "friends of school libraries" that can fund-raise for the library.

Fund-raising events such as book fairs directly reflect the mission of the library and they are repeatable, provide visibility, and promote goodwill and loyalty. Participants will put the event in their calendars and plan to attend well ahead of time.

Two words of caution: 1) You must make sure your friends' group is in charge of these activities or you may find yourself in this role rather than the role for which you were hired. 2) Many organizations in the community, as well as other parts of the school itself, are involved in fund-raising. You don't want to be in competition with the Parent Teacher Organization, the cheerleaders, or the band wishing to earn money to march in New York's St. Patrick's Day Parade. You need to position your effort at a different time than these others. For some ideas, both traditional and creative, to raise funds, see Appendix A.

Don't be discouraged if your team's first efforts to raise money are not as successful as you have hoped. You've heard the adage to "try, try, again." Do a little assessment. Did you expect too much? Do you have the right audience for the type of fund-raising? Rethink, start with a small step, and then build. You could just tell students that because you don't charge fines for overdue materials, you would like to have a "Pennies (or nickels) for fines" day where each classroom will collect coins and you can use them.

Your School Library Budget

Once you know how much money you have to spend, it is important to carefully budget so that your dollars go as far as possible. Most principals will ask for a library budget or give you an amount and ask for an accounting of how it will be spent. When planning your budget, be sure to consider each of these major portions of a typical school library program and spell out exactly where you will and won't be able to spend money. Include line items with zeroes to show exactly where your budget is lacking.

Collection

Books
Electronic resources
Magazines/journals
Nonprint (Videos, DVDs, CDs)

Furniture and Equipment

Computers
Copier
Laminating machine
Seating
Shelving

Professional Development

Conference
Seminar
User groups

Programming

    After school reading tutor
    Book clubs
    Battle of the Books
    Reading Incentive Programs
    Special events
    Theme nights
    Young reader medal activities

Technology

    Upgrade costs to hardware/software
    Maintenance
    New equipment; hardware, software, peripherals
    Service agreements

Supplies

    Book jackets and adhesive paperback covering
    Book repair materials
    Die cuts
    Laminating film
    Paper
    Pencils
    Spine labels
    Tape
    Printer cartridges/toner

Administrators appreciate school librarians that are conscientious about spending wisely to provide programs and services that support the mission of the school.

Notes

1. Find more information about the Improving Literacy Through School Libraries grant at http://www.ed.gov/programs/lsl/index.html.

2. All funding data from the U.S. Dept. of Education, http://www.ed.gov/programs/lsl/funding.html. Accessed December 4, 2009.

CHAPTER 8

The ProACTive Librarian

School librarians have always been wise to be proACTive. These are the times when it is no longer an option. School libraries are being threatened at budget time with the loss of some if not all staffing. Any hope of purchasing new resources or equipment is in jeopardy. Other remedies include having the school librarian teach an academic subject using the library as the classroom, halting any use by other students. Ignoring the situation and hoping a miracle will happen is not likely. It's time to ACT.

Ten "ProACTive" Action Items for Every School Librarian

Do:

✓ Get out your calendar and write down the dates and times of your school board meetings, city council meetings, county board of education meetings, and any other decision-making group gatherings
✓ Start a success journal where you write down the everyday successes that are so hard to remember when you are put on the spot
✓ Locate your state and local representatives and add them to your address book; include e-mail addresses, office addresses, and phone numbers
✓ Research your contacts—read the back issues of the legislative section in your state school library/library association
✓ Sign up on a Listserv of school librarians and read them on a regular basis
✓ Attend the legislative day or day in the district planned by your state association
✓ Find out what is important to the local decision-makers by getting your hands on (and reading) the professional literature that they are reading
✓ Learn the language and terminology that decision-makers are using, understand their concerns, and offer solutions by linking the success of the school library program to answering those concerns
✓ Join the team: be a part of the whole school leadership team, if you belong to an association; join the legislative committee
✓ Offer solutions that show creative use of the library staff and space when the school encounters a problem that seems unsolvable

Our definitions:

proactive

1. Acting in advance to deal with an expected change or difficulty. *The proactive school librarian wears many hats.*
2. Controlling a situation by causing something to happen rather than waiting to respond to it after it happens. *The new movie brought in a crowd of girls asking for the book, and the proactive librarian had plenty of copies ready.*

Proactive Quiz

Use the rubric to chart your progress in each area. Circle or underline the one that best describes you.

	At-Risk	Making Progress	Satisfactory	Exemplary
District	I am uncertain who makes the decisions about the level of staffing and library budget.	I know who makes the decisions about libraries, but I am not able to communicate with these people.	I know and communicate with those who make decisions about school library service. I attend school board meetings when the agenda has items regarding school libraries.	I personally know and communicate often with those who make library decisions. I attend school board meetings when the agenda has items regarding school libraries. I serve in an advisory capacity within the district regarding library service.
Local	I am uncertain of the local government in my area.	I know the names of the mayor, city council members, and city staff. I do not attend meetings, however.	I attend occasional city council meetings and feel comfortable inviting these local dignitaries to school library events.	I personally know and meet with local dignitaries on a variety of issues. I attend occasional city council meetings, and local dignitaries have visited my school library.
County	I've never been to the county Office of	There are limited opportunities to attend	I regularly attend county Office of Education	I have met with county officials regarding

	At-Risk	Making Progress	Satisfactory	Exemplary
	Education or there are no contacts for libraries there.	county Office of Education events and board meetings, but I occasionally participate.	events, and know the board of supervisors addresses and contact people.	issues that affect school libraries. I participate in countywide and county-sponsored library events.
State	I am unaware of any state legislation that affects school libraries and am unsure about contacting my representatives.	I have written, called by phone, or e-mailed my state representative and keep track of pending legislation that affects school libraries.	I have visited my state representatives. I am aware of the legislative issues regarding school libraries.	I have visited my state representatives. I am aware of the legislative issues regarding school libraries. I am part of a legislative network that initiates grassroots action when threatening issues loom.
National	I am unaware of my senators and representatives.	I have written, called by phone, or e-mailed my national-level representatives.	I have visited my national-level representative regarding school library issues.	I have visited my national-level representatives regarding school library issues. I am part of a national network that initiates grassroots action when legislation is pending.
Initiative	I am unable to get started and overwhelmed by lack of a concrete, step-by-step menu to follow. I'm looking for a mentor.	I have done some reading about advocacy and feel ready to start. I have at least made initial contact. When speaking about the importance of school libraries, I am	I initiate meetings to communicate a message filled with evidence from experts and student-created products that represent their learning.	During meetings with legislators, I am able to bring multiple perspectives to show the importance of school libraries to parents, teachers, students, and administrators. I have asked

(Continued)

	At-Risk	Making Progress	Satisfactory	Exemplary
		nervous and tongue-tied.		the legislator to reassess their positions based on evidence I provided, and received assurances that this person is a supporter.
Collaboration with others on advocacy	I make no attempt to communicate with legislators and decision-makers. Instead, I rely on the advocacy efforts of my colleagues and those in professional organizations.	I contact legislators on my own, but do not wish to collaborate with my colleagues or those advocating through professional organizations.	I collaborate with one or two of my colleagues or participate in legislative advocacy efforts through a professional organization.	I collaborate with a variety of colleagues and professional associations in formal advocacy efforts and share new insights into issues through this process.
Understanding and communicating the issues	My knowledge and expertise on school libraries is limited, and I have trouble relating what I do know because of nervousness.	My knowledge and expertise on the importance of school libraries is evident, but my arguments are based on opinion, anecdotal evidence, or emotions.	My knowledge and expertise is evident, and the information I pass on is clear, appropriate, and correct.	My knowledge and expertise is evident to the extent that decision-makers seek me out for advice. I present clear, appropriate, and compelling arguments that connect the layman to the intricacies of the school library-academic-achievement connection.
Showing ... not just telling	When I bring something to demonstrate my points, the decision-makers don't	The product I bring matches its purpose and intent, but is not well organized or does	The product I bring achieves its purpose, and the intended audience is	The product I bring matches its purpose, intent, and intended audience. The

At-Risk	Making Progress	Satisfactory	Exemplary
understand its purpose or intent. I tend to be drawn off-topic and can be distracted from the message I am trying to communicate.	not hold the interest of the audience.	interested. This may or may not persuade decision-makers to take a firm stance.	product is organized, holds the interest of the audience, and clearly states a call to action, which the decision-makers agree to support or research.

To begin being proactive, start by focusing on what you love, the smile when a student returns with a book and wants another one just like it. Remember the awe on the face of students who view the front page of the *New York Times* printed on the day they were born. Notice the faces as you tell a story to kindergarten children.

Think about the many reasons you decided to work in a school library. Your school librarians were so effective that you wished to emulate them. In some cases, your mother, father, aunt, or uncle was a school librarian and you wanted to follow in their footsteps.

What you learn every day are the intangible rewards that come with being an exceptional school librarian, from the affection of the students to the gratefulness of the teachers and maybe even the admiration of the administrator. You have learned to engage in a wide variety of tasks that keep the library environment fresh, appealing, and energizing. You have the perfect opportunity to influence the whole school, instilling a love of reading, a desire to find information, and a dedication to learning.

Some may have arrived by happenstance, but you have recognized that you are the one who has the capacity to turn the school library as a classroom into a place that inspires and uplifts those who enter it. It is a profession that makes a difference for your school community and ultimately how people feel about and access libraries beyond your school. Even with the challenges that you will face fighting for your program, your work truly does have a positive impact for your students, their families, and the future.

The School Librarian: Agent of Change

The world is constantly changing, with new, promising technologies forecast to revolutionize the world of books and libraries as they exist today. You cannot keep doing the same programs and services that have been the mainstay of school library service and hope that decision-makers will value and fund them. Enhanced catalogs with personalization features, electronic access 24/7, electronic reading devices and e-books, and tracking textbooks and teaching materials are just a few examples of change that adds value to the school community. Whether or not you embrace all or any of the changes that are asked of you may very well save your position and your program. Understanding the changing world of the school librarian and what it means for students, teachers, and parents is basic to the advocacy that must happen at the local, county, state, and federal level.

Many schools and school libraries need radical change. The philosophies of the past must be examined to make sure that the school library, as a space and a resource, is still relevant and necessary. Change is something that school librarians must embrace because it not only relates to the continuation of their positions, but it is a noble thing to want to make the world a better place. The school librarian can enable students and teachers to do more or to find new and better ways to do things.

The change that is needed is not just that you must change something, but that you must help others to accept and incorporate the new, the different, and sometimes the difficult. Not everyone is ready for small changes, not to mention radical ones. Some school librarians may wax rhapsodic about the good old days of the card catalog and silent libraries, or complain about how this new generation is only interested in computers, but those days are gone, never to return. Being out of synch with the electronic age and dragging your feet about adopting new technologies will inevitably lead others to view the library as an anachronism. Students and teachers have no interest in spending time and effort doing something the old way when they can find what they want and need more quickly and easily themselves.

How can you measure if you are ready to be an agent of change or stand as a roadblock to progress? What sort of changes are you ready to undertake? Specifically, are you making changes that involve your role, your environment, or the basic processes and policies of the library?

Challenge yourself to look closely at your position and programs as they exist now, and what it is you'd like to change, and then analyze what you must change to provide the twenty-first-century skills your students must have when they leave your school at whatever level. You must convince yourself that you have both the will and the capability to change before you can ask others to do the same.

You will need to examine your own motives for the changes you propose. Will these changes make your job easier so that you can provide more services? Change may be critical to increase your personal power and prestige so that you can implement activities that will be beneficial to others. When your principal recognizes that you are a driving force in improving education in your school, you will have the ability to make changes that matter.

Understanding people and providing a mechanism for them to benefit from changes you make must be central to your motivation to change. When you change things that you do, but it doesn't make any appreciable positive difference for the people who use the library, then the change was irrelevant.

Changes may require money, time, or space, and these are not easy to acquire in a time of economic downturns. If these are the only changes that will help, you will need to concentrate on how to raise the money, take the time, and make the space to do this.

What roles are you willing to have? The change agent must wear a lot of hats! You must be the cheerleader who makes noise when change is announced and also when it yields results. You must be the counselor who lets others know that it is okay to accept these changes and explain the why and how and when. You must be the salesperson who overcomes the objections of others to change. You must be the coach who encourages others to embrace change so that it is incorporated into the culture of the school.

Do you focus on the future rather than the present? The school librarian who is an agent of change has a vision of what could be or should be. The librarian adheres to this vision regardless of the current state of affairs and is ready to overcome major obstacles. In some sense, the librarian knows that there is something better waiting to be built, found, learned, or incorporated. The change agent explores alternatives rather than clinging to the tradition of "this is how it's always been done." This basic dissatisfaction with the status quo, even when things are satisfactory in the eyes of others, is the trademark quality of school librarians ready for change. The agent of change will not accept being taken for granted or discounted by others, but will persevere in efforts to keep library service essential to the academic endeavors of both students and faculty.

Does your passion for school libraries inspire others? School librarians must have a passion for their role, a passion so inspirational that it may lead others to become information professionals. This passion translates into always working to achieve the best that can be offered in your library. This has the aspect of the need to change, and you must be ready for and desire change and must have a tremendous amount of stamina to repeatedly make arguments that will persuade others willing to invest in that change. Without passion for your vision, your program will remain stagnant and could be easily dismantled. Your passion allows you to look at problems and consider solutions and to engage others.

Advocacy as a Planned Activity

A formal advocacy program for school libraries requires a committed group of people from many different stakeholder groups willing to speak to decision-makers about the essential nature of the school library. It takes time and effort to schedule meetings, arm others with compelling information to share, and jump through the myriad hoops that stand in the way of making those personal connections with people who are busy, important, and possibly located far away. The overall objective of this advocacy program is to ensure that decision-makers understand the school library system and how their decisions/actions affect it, and to get a commitment from them to work toward strong school libraries. Advocacy takes many forms, from marketing within the school to visiting decision-makers and legislators. It also means writing letters to the editor of your local newspaper, using technology to spread your message, and contacting legislators.

School librarians must instruct parents, teachers, and students who wish to advocate for the library program by giving them information about the impact of strong school libraries and the statistics you have gathered showing the impact your program has on teaching and learning in your school. It is important, though, not to send them in with a canned message that seems insincere. We can empower others to speak for themselves from their hearts. This will generate more goodwill than having them recite a speech we wrote for them with only our own views and opinions in it. They must repackage your information into something they can say sincerely. Students and teachers can speak from their own experiences when you help them document these activities.

Advocacy efforts include a focus on legislation and influencing decision-makers and marketing the library program. School librarians can and should visit decision-makers. Bringing students, teachers, and parents along can help you state your case without seeming self-promoting. If you only visit a decision-maker when you need something or want to protest something, you may find yourself treated as an adversary. If you make regular visits just to help the decision-maker understand change in your program, over time you can build relationships by seeking common ground. This is discussed in more detail below.

Your marketing plan includes advertising, public relations, and promotions. Advertising is how you may attract students, parents, and teachers into the library. Bulletin boards, posters, newsletters, displays, and announcements are common advertising mediums for school libraries. Promotions could include announcements of your upcoming book fair or could feature new additions to the library collection. It might be a special display of student work you are featuring in the library, or it could be plans for a display of books and materials for Black History Month, President's Day, or the Newbery/Caldecott/Coretta Scott King winners, with the most recent announcements featured.

Once your patrons begin increasing their visits, it is important to have good public-relations policies. Setting positive relationships with patrons is the goal so that they become repeat visitors. Your public-relations program is important because it sets the stage for promoting regular programming and special events when you want to draw a crowd.

Ten Good Ideas for Advocacy Meetings

These are good rules to use all the time, but especially as you interact with others during official visits, making presentations to groups, or speaking at meetings.

1. Come in with the expectation that you are going to be successful and don't apologize for taking the time of others.
2. Approach this opportunity with some experience, not as a cold appearance. If you are going to speak at a board meeting, go to a few and observe first. What is the protocol, and how will you be treated?
3. Listen before talking if you engage in a conversation. See if you can establish common ground before you ask for something.
4. Don't waste the time of others because you will find them avoiding you in the future. Get to the point (quickly) and make your case. Do not repeat the same information. If you want to add emphasis to your argument, tell a story that illustrates what you mean.
5. Use new and exciting presentations rather than falling into the trap of doing an old, tired presentation. You may have created a PowerPoint that was once informative and convincing, but it will fall short if you use it with the wrong audience, recite it by rote, or fail to read the reaction of the audience and adjust your presentation.
6. Respect the people you are addressing even if you disapprove of or disagree with their positions and decisions in the past. Disrespect and blame will alienate them. If you are asking for their help, you must keep that relationship door open and allow them to proceed with dignity.
7. Find out if there will be something in it for the group you are addressing. Seldom will you get support for something that does not benefit the person or group in some way. For your district decision-makers, this can be higher test scores, more students staying in school to graduate, and better behavior because students are happier at school. For your legislators, it will mean good visibility to constituents, especially parents, who want their children to have good schools.
8. Celebrate when you are successful, and remember to go back and say thank you. Say it publicly, if possible, so that you can return for support in the future.
9. Keep a positive attitude. Don't give up if you aren't successful at first. Don't feel guilty or embarrassed if your voice shakes or you stumble through your first presentations. Public speaking gets easier the more you do it.
10. Take supporters with you because there is strength in numbers. Standing up by yourself in front of a "new" audience or group such as the school board or service organization is easier if you have others with you to lend strength to your cause, especially if those include parents and students.

Legislative Visits

Personal visits are an effective way of engaging elected officials on issues important to school libraries. Legislators are extremely busy, but they do want to meet their constituents and will take time to meet you if you plan a visit in advance. The best time to schedule a visit to their "official" office is on a day set aside for you by the legislators when they are in session. This is more easily done when you are attending a special day with one or more professional associations. Their offices are generally in the same building or adjacent buildings and you can visit many of them in one day. Again, strength in numbers is generally an advantage, and you might consider visiting with public librarians or teachers. It can be difficult to attend these days if they occur on a day when you can't miss work, or if the trip would cost more than you can afford. Do not despair; you have an alternative that can be just as effective.

Big states, like Alaska, Arizona, California, New Mexico, and Texas, may require several hundred miles of travel to visit the state capital. It may be better to make an appointment at their home office when the legislature is not in session. If this is your first visit, invite someone to come with you, preferably a board member or someone who is already known to the legislator. However, this isn't a requirement. Another librarian in your district or a parent can go with you.

Even with advance planning and appointments, you may find yourself talking to staff members rather than the person you want to see. You will have a better chance of getting to see the actual person if you are on time, prepared, and polite. You will have a short time, usually an hour or less, to make your points, so be ready with what you want to say. At all times, remember that this is a visit to promote school libraries. If you have differing opinions on other issues, this is not the time to discuss them. You are on a positive mission for schools and school libraries and you want the staff or the legislator to listen. It is important to stay focused so your efforts aren't dismissed because you are talking about something other than what is relevant to your visit.

Introduce everyone who is visiting and explain your purpose for the meeting. Elected officials have a philosophy, party lines, and an agenda, and you should do your research in advance to find where they stand on issues of schools, libraries, and other related legislative issues. It is not necessary to enlighten them to your way of thinking with a brief visit. You want to influence what they do, not what they believe, so you need to adapt your approach to the person you are speaking with by appealing to his or her self-interest. Take a fact sheet about your school library and what you need or want. Thank the legislator for his or her time and leave the fact sheet with your contact information.

Libraries and education are full of acronyms and technical terms that you will want to avoid using unless your legislator is sure to know and understand them. Take the comments and questions of the person you are visiting seriously, and write down notes so that you can remember later what you covered. If you don't know the answer to a question, say that you'll find out. Then do the research and get answers back quickly. Send a thank-you note within a week of your visit, and make sure to include the information that you promised. When issues are presented during the legislative session, you can send a note or e-mail referring to your meeting and asking for help.

Making Yourself Memorable

Pick a theme and use it in all your communications. Get others from your area to use this same theme. For example, School Library Systems (state of New York) recommends in its advocacy toolkit:[1]

Be a part of a sunflower avalanche to get your message noticed! School libraries make the sun shine on everyone!

- Use yellow paper for testimony forms in the advocacy toolkit.
- Use sunflower images and sunflower stationery links below to get the attention of our budget decision-makers.
- Share the good news of equity, access, success! [This is their slogan.]
- Write letters, e-mail, call, or visit your legislators and legislative leaders.
- Convey the real world of school libraries and school library systems and their value for learners.

Sunflowers are a great symbol for the state of Florida, but search for a symbol that is relevant to your situation. The goal is to make your communication efforts *memorable*. You want them to remember your message after you leave their office, after you send a letter, and even if you are just touching base via e-mail.

What Is Your Message?

You obviously have many different reasons for advocating for strong school libraries, but you need to focus on those that are most important for your present situation. Some message ideas are below. Can you add five more of your own?

- Aside from their school library, many students have no other source for free reading materials they can take home.
- Information-literacy instruction and assistance with research (and the research process) must be introduced early by a school librarian and reinforced every year thereafter. Students must have sufficient practice at using these skills. This requires a well-developed scope and sequence of activities done in collaboration with classroom teachers.
- School libraries are not simply cost centers on the campus, they are the best way to maximize the investment in technology and books. The skillful management of textbooks and teacher materials can save a substantial amount over the life of an adoption. Instead of providing small clusters of computers that often do not get used, the library houses large groupings of computers so that instruction in a lab-style environment is possible. The library allows access to all students and teachers, which reduces the need to duplicate these titles in each and every classroom.

- School libraries are about equity and access. School libraries must be open at the time that students need them. They should be open for the entirety of the instructional day, as well as before and after school. Students who are not given access to these resources will be at a great disadvantage when they are expected to perform at the same academic level as students who do.
- School librarians are experts in locating, evaluating, and using information and resources for teachers and students and are the educators who teach these critical skills to students.
- School library collections must be maintained consistently, including collection development by a teacher-librarian, effective weeding, and access to well-chosen electronic subscription services. Even a well-stocked library can become quickly out of date if there is no materials budget for a sustained period.
- School libraries provide the environment for learning that emulates real-world problem-solving and lifelong learning: critical thinking, collaboration, written communication, information technology, creativity, ethics and social responsibility, self-direction, oral communication, and a strong work ethic.
- Services that are provided in the school library cannot be duplicated elsewhere, do not happen in the regular classroom, and are directly related to the academic success of students. This is especially true for advanced students who need enrichment opportunities and students who need strategic intervention and nonstandard resources.
- School librarians are leaders on campus in technology, staff development, instruction, and literacy.
- School librarians increase student achievement.
- The school library is the largest classroom in the school, shared by all students and teachers, and as such, a full-time school librarian who is also a teacher should be dedicated to it.
- At the present time and until all students have access to all online resources, the school library must have adequate technology and bandwidth to accommodate large groups of students needing to do advanced research.

Elevator Pitches

Based on the idea that you may get a very short time (such as a ride in an elevator) with a very important person, this pitch is the most powerful, concise description of the importance of school libraries meant to spark an interest in continuing the discussion further. An elevator ride is very short. The reason to have an elevator pitch ready is not just because you might actually use it in an elevator, but because you must look at all the ideas you want to share and focus in on the most important ideas bringing you to the core of your message.

The examples below are very short. You may want to expand them with your own words to fit your situation.

- The library is the critical link to building engaged, proficient readers.
- Many of our students don't have books and computers in their homes, so the library gives them access to rich resources in our collection and electronically to the world.

- The library is where students learn information-literacy skills essential to success in school and life in the twenty-first century.
- The library is the thriving heart of the school where students pursue learning on topics of their own choosing, rather than simply learning content required by the state, teacher, or high-stakes testing.

Write your own elevator speech! You can find lots of cut-and-paste samples on the Internet, and you may even find a script by an association. With this in mind, try to find a way to own your pitch by making sure your voice rings true or tells the story. Without sounding like an encyclopedia, you do need to have something based on facts and numbers and not on suppositions. Focus on the current opportunities or problems that exist in education and how school libraries provide value and solutions. Don't be afraid to say that there are costs, benefits, and returns on investment in education that are similar to those in the corporate world.

Practice your pitch until it sounds natural and easy, and time it. You need to convey the importance of your message through a passionate, confident delivery. If it is longer than 40 seconds, then you must trim it down and decide what is really the core message and what is superfluous. When you've gotten the pitch perfected, it is time to memorize it and try it out on colleagues, family, and friends. Take their constructive criticism and make your pitch even better.

Letter-Writing Campaigns

Legislators at all levels vote on behalf of their constituents, so letters are one important way to let them know which legislation to support. They usually pay attention to letters, postcards, faxes, and e-mail communications. The more items they receive on a topic, the more seriously they will take the input. Often, the legislator does not have the time to personally read letters, but assigns this to an assistant. The assistant may simply give the tally of for and against or highlight excerpts of letters for the legislator to read later. However, the critical point here is that there are numbers to tally. Legislators are often asked to vote on a measure for which they have had no response at all from the people most affected it.

Remember that you are asking them for help, so be polite and persuasive. Your purpose for writing should be stated in a regarding line or in the first paragraph of the letter. Keep your remarks limited to the one issue, and try to keep the letter short. Use stories and personal experiences to illustrate your message. Use the name of the pending legislation (AB200, SB546, HR3240, etc.).

- Have school library advocates pass out a stack of postcards with suggested wording for adults willing to help. All that has to be done is to fill in and sign the postcards.

- Give presentations about a legislative issue that will impact the school library at a meeting or seminar. Conclude the presentation by asking those moved to do so to send a postcard or letter. Have legislator names and addresses as well as key points available, but have them complete their own handwritten letters before they leave. You may want to provide stamps for their envelopes and offer to mail them.
- Get permission from parents to film students using the school library. Let students help you edit the video, and have it playing at events like back-to-school night and open house. Have addresses and letter-writing materials available so that parents can easily write down the valuable things they see. You could even send a copy of the video to the legislator.
- Partner with the public library and set up tables at local festivals, fairs, or community events. Speak with everyone willing to listen as they pass by. Lure them over with bookmarks or books, and invite them to write a letter or fill out a postcard.
- Ask your school board to send a letter in support of proposed legislation.
- Almost any local organization could help support your issue: chamber of commerce, service organizations, city councils, executive boards, etc.

Sample Letter

Date:

Re: Support for SB000 "School Library Collection Development Grant"

Dear _____,

   I am writing in support of funding SB000, a law establishing a grant program to support public school libraries in the state of _____. As a parent, I know the importance of having a school library staffed with a credentialed library teacher and stocked with adequate resources for educating and engaging students.

   This law would help all school libraries to purchase books, magazines, reference materials, and electronic databases, as well as additional computers. This law will also free up funds to provide wireless Internet access in the library.

   I am asking you to make this smart investment to promote the promise of free and open access to school libraries for all K–12 _____ students and their families. As the economic crisis worsens, I see more and more of my neighbors needing access to the school library to use the computers. They are looking for jobs, information about refinancing their homes, and access to social services.

   I know that you care about this issue, but I also know that budgetary strains could mean that you won't be able to fund certain programs. I'm asking that you please make sure strong school library programs continue for the students and families who need them most.

   Please act now to ensure that more, not fewer, students have access to the resources they need to become twenty-first-century learners.

   I appreciate your leadership on this important issue,

   Signature

Letters to the Editor

Which letters are printed in newspapers in the letters to the editor section? Usually short ones that make one point and make it well. If you are a regular newspaper reader, keep your eyes peeled for related articles about schools, test scores, literacy, technology, and libraries in general. Does the article spark an idea for you to write about? Is there something fundamentally missing, wrong, or misleading about the article? For example, if there is an article about the dip in reading scores, and the school library is not mentioned in the article, then you have a perfect opportunity to write a letter to the editor pointing out the omission and the probable connection.

The quickest way to get your letter to the attention of the editor is to e-mail your submission. Make sure that it contains no misspellings or grammatical errors. Read it aloud to be sure that it flows logically and sounds natural. In your letter, state the article or argument to which you're responding, then detail your own position and refer to at least a few pieces of evidence in favor of your view. Close with a quick restatement of your position and sign it with your name, address, and contact information.

Using Technology to Spread Your Message

At a minimum, there should be something on the school library Web page that references the importance of the school library. It could be a slogan, an article, or a letter from a grateful teacher or student. Having pictures of students engaged in activities that support academic achievement is one easy way to make the point; students working on a collaborative project, consulting reference books, using the computer, reading, or keying their reports. Remember that, although many students have very public Facebook pages, not all do, and you should make sure you have parents' permission to showcase their child's image on your Web site.

You may have other options to use technology to spread the message. Find out what students and teachers are using. Explore new programs on a regular basis. Some of them will be great and some will be flops.

Blogs

Keeping a journal about the happenings in the school library is a good way of capturing those fleeting moments that best illustrate the importance of what happens there. Use a Weblog service such as Blogger or Blogspot to make your journaling easy and accessible to others.

Book-Lover Sites

Don't forget about GoodReads, LibraryThing, and Shelfari. You don't need to re-create your catalog here; however, you can help students create their own home library catalog there and keep lists of things they have read to easily get recommendations of other things to read. This is a great way for librarians to learn what others are reading, what they want to read, and to inform collection development.

Listservs

Subscribe and post to Listservs, which are electronic mailing lists that allow easy distribution of e-mail to a large group of interested participants. A Listserv could even be set up for teachers, parents, and students to allow easy distribution of information about library events and programs.

Microblogging

Use a Web application such as Twitter to send and read text-based messages, generally on cell phones and personal computers. Let patrons know that they can sign up as subscribers (or followers). It is a quick and easy way to get out the word when you have an upcoming event or need volunteers.

Photo Sharing

Instead of putting your pictures in photo albums that get little use in the library, post all your pictures electronically on Web applications like Flickr, Photobucket, and Picasa. Try Animoto to set a slideshow of pictures to music. The transitions, movement, and zooms are all done for you. You'll end up with an upbeat, slick presentation visually showcasing your library.

Podcasting/Webcasting

You can record voice messages on a variety of products, such as iTunes, to send out short or long sound recordings on a regular basis. Try Voice-Thread to capture group conversations to share with others via the Internet. This application also allows you to create a collaborative multimedia slide show that holds sound, images, documents, and video. Once you've edited your VoiceThread into the final product, you can promote it by providing a link to it on your Web page, sending out e-mail announcements about it, and asking others to view it and make comments.

Presentations

Narrate your PowerPoint or Keynote presentation and post it online for people to view at their leisure. Include pictures and video and keep it brief. Capture your elevator speech and make it perfect by including student narration, teacher comments, or work products created in the library.

Social Networks

You can set up an account on Facebook, MySpace, Ning, and virtually dozens of others so that patrons can visit to find out more about the library program. Most of these allow you to solicit fans and you can update the live feed with current reminders about events. Find out the social network that the teachers and students are using most and set it up there.

Wikis

Keep a wiki as a collaborative space to allow others to contribute to your cause. This can be a place to store final student work products, documents, evidence, or any file/link. You can also use this space to allow brainstorming of ideas for ways the library can do even more to support students and teachers.

Coalitions

Nothing is more powerful than several groups of people working toward a common goal. Other organizations with areas of overlap make great opportunities for partnerships, both long-lasting and issue-specific. School library organizations can find out when other organizations have their annual conference and make sure there is a table with information and a working librarian to answer questions. Some strong organizations for school librarians to partner with are listed below.

- School board associations: School board associations can support national or statewide initiatives such as Reading Every Day, Equal Access to Libraries, or One Book projects.
- P-T-S organizations: Parents, teachers, and students are often members of the PTA, PTSA, or PTO at your school and the state or national organization. The power of bringing them on board lies in the vast reach of their voice. Getting their support for the library is an important step in building a base of people who will speak up for you when it is needed.
- Other library associations: Libraries of all kinds have many areas of overlapping concern. Reach out to public libraries, college and university libraries, and other local libraries to see if you have some common goals. Work together to achieve them.
- Teacher associations: Teachers have special areas of interest. They belong to a wide variety of associations that may partner with school library associations to write grants, achieve common objectives, and cosponsor events. If your school has a particular focus toward a specific topic, like a magnet school, that association would be a good place to seek partnerships.
- Unions.
- Literacy teachers.
- Teachers of reading, social studies, science, foreign language, English, music, and art.

- Technology teachers.
- Nonprofit organizations.
    o Early childhood focused groups.
    o Reading and literacy focused groups.
    o Foundations.

Begin by attending as many meetings of decision-making groups as possible to learn the culture and focus of each. When your job or programs are threatened, you can then approach the proper group for support and resolution. Remember to be passionate about the aspects you love about your job and be an agent of change for your school. Meet regularly with your legislators for they are the ones who can make mandates about library service. Make your communications memorable by using a theme or common message. Create an elevator speech so that you are ready when you get a chance to talk to someone who can help you in your cause. Use letter-writing campaigns and submit letters to the editor to get your goals noticed by a larger group of people. Use technology to spread your message quickly and without high costs. Join or start partnerships or coalitions to join forces with other groups.

Note

1. School Library Systems, http://www.crbsls.org/slsa/. Accessed December 22, 2009.

CHAPTER 9

The ReACTive Librarian

Despite your best efforts and those of your supporters, you receive the dreaded "pink slip," generally in the form of a reduction-in-force letter or a notice that you have been reassigned to a different position. Luckily, this is usually not a final sentence, and there is still time to react to save your position and program. You may not be able to control the decisions that are being made, but you can control how you react.

Ten "ReACTive" Action Items for Every School Librarian

Do:

✓ Have a library supporter ready to gather signatures from students, teachers, and parents to petition decisions that reduce library services
✓ Continue to do your job to the best of your ability during the hours you are paid, and keep advocacy efforts to your personal time
✓ Create message statements about the importance of the library and what may be lost—double check every message to be sure it is about students or teachers and not librarians
✓ Read everything that is given to you by your principal, by your union, and by your district And follow instructions carefully so that you do not lose your position to a legal technicality
✓ Keep copies of documents and communications you are sent and stay organized so that all of it is easily retrievable should you need to reference anything quickly
✓ Attend school board meetings
✓ Talk to others in the same situation and coordinate advocacy activities so that your efforts aren't duplicated
✓ Find a support group filled with others not involved in your situation so that you have a safe place to talk, complain, and get sympathy
✓ Don't give up, remain positive and hopeful—decisions can be changed
✓ Start making a realistic back-up plan in case you are not successful

Our definitions:

reactive

1. Having a response to a situation or threat. *A librarian who receives a reduction-in-force notice must be quickly reactive.*
2. Occurring as a result of stress or emotional upset, especially from factors outside the control of the person/organization. *A reactive librarian may do more harm than good by lashing out against the very people they later need to ask for help.*

Reactivity Quiz

Fill in the blanks with the answers most appropriate to your situation.

1. Write down the names and titles of the chain of command from your direct supervisor up through each level of management to the superintendent or school board.

   _____

   _____

   _____

2. The most respected person associated with our district is _____ .
3. Who wields the greatest financial power? _____
4. Who decides what will happen in the libraries? _____
5. Who is in charge of the district-level technical responsibilities for the online catalog and circulation system? _____
6. Who writes the district's library plan or sets long-term goals for the library program? _____
7. Who initiates meetings for library staff? _____
8. Who creates the agenda for district-wide library meetings? _____
9. Who chairs the meetings that I am required to attend? _____
10. Who completes your evaluation? _____
11. Who is the president of your parent-teacher organization? _____
12. Who is the student-council president? _____

Quiz results:

You should have been able to fill in the blanks fairly quickly. These are the people for your crisis-communication mailing list. You should send letters explaining the situation and asking for their help. Sample letters are included later in this chapter.

Foreshadowing

Don't be under the delusion that a person or position is irreplaceable. Administrators come and go with their own prejudices, goals, and ideas about how they will improve their school(s). Sometimes this includes legislation such as No Child Left Behind or research-based evidence that directs them to make decisions that are counterintuitive to what school librarians and teachers know about students and literacy.

Before you receive the dreaded reduction-in-force letter, there are generally many signs that your position might not be safe. Even so, it is not uncommon to hear school librarians say that they were blindsided by their principal or by the district when their position was eliminated. Generally, these are not last-minute decisions, but rather a topic that has been carefully debated and considered by management. Rarely are these decisions kept completely quiet. People on your campus may serve in an advisory capacity, and they have been charged to keep things confidential. These persons or circle of people may give unintended clues during interactions with you.

School librarians must have a clear idea of what they do and how this fits into the culture of the school and district. They must always have their ear to the ground and nose to the wind so that they know what is happening. Ask judicious, careful questions of people who can be trusted when rumors surface. Don't spread information that hasn't been officially confirmed. It is easy to be written off as paranoid if you overreact to signs that you have misread, but then again, you don't want to ignore a situation if the writing is on the wall.

Do you have ostrich syndrome? Definition: denying or refusing to acknowledge something that is blatantly obvious as if your head were in the sand like an ostrich.[1]

Signs that your position is in jeopardy:

- You are not involved at the same level as previously with what is going on at your school, especially in terms of planning for next year. You have been forgotten or uninvited to important school-wide meetings. You are no longer having discussions with the principal or teaching staff about what you'll need to do in the library for next year. When you propose an idea for next year, you get a noncommittal answer or the topic is changed. You are sent to trainings that seem to have no connection with the library program and told that your attendance is mandatory.
- People are avoiding you, and are uncomfortable making small talk. When you enter a room, the conversation stops or changes. People seem to be whispering more often in your presence. You are not being invited to social events when most of the other teachers attend, and they may make no effort to keep these activities quiet in order to protect your feelings.
- Others dislike you on campus and it is well known that they would be happy if you were gone.
- You are being assigned tasks that are beyond your capacity to do effectively (not enough time, outside the scope of your job, or without a budget) and you have no possibility of a successful outcome. This could also include being assigned to a special project that takes you away from your usual duties.

- Alternatively, you are given ever-increasingly less responsibility. You are asked to train others to do extra nonlibrary duties such as overseeing student council, running the student store, or supervising the crosswalk patrol program. This is especially telling if you are not given other additional duties in the place of this.
- You see that tasks that are reserved for your position have been added to other job descriptions. If you have been responsible for collection development, purchasing, and processing new acquisitions, you should be concerned if selection and purchasing are now the responsibility of a district-level person and processing is included as a new task for clerks or technicians.
- You have been out on leave for an extended time (such as for maternity, disability or injury, or surgery) and you have received comments that everything went on perfectly in your absence.
- You did not get your scheduled pay increase because of a poor evaluation. A major problem on your campus was either your responsibility or something that you caused or were somehow involved in. You were formally counseled about areas that need improvement or you were referred to a person for peer assistance.
- Oral communication with your superior has stopped, and now is occurring primarily in ways that can be used as documentation. E-mails and notes from your superior are written in a tone that indicates dissatisfaction or irritation.
- You were asked to explain your procedures for dealing with money collection. Are you being asked to make a second accounting for money that was accounted for and turned into the proper channels?
- City-wide rumors suggest that the school may be closed, renamed, or taken over by the state or a charter. The principal is being reassigned or fired, and anyone aligned with this administrator will be facing reassignment.
- The library is left off a school-improvements list. Air-conditioning installation, carpet cleaning, repainting, and other repairs are occurring everywhere else except the library.

Getting the Bad News

One of the most difficult things that can happen to a school librarian is getting the official notice that your library is being closed or that you are being laid off, reassigned to a nonlibrary job, or reduced in hours. Although not as life-disrupting, you may be caught off-guard if you find that your position is safe but someone with more seniority is taking it and you are being bumped to another location. The information about your position may come through a discussion with your administrator, a phone call from human resources, or a group meeting with all affected participants. If you are being reassigned, it may not affect your salary or benefits and the process will seem fairly unofficial. Before you make the decision to react, you must decide if the effort will be worth the probable outcome.

If you are being laid off, the news is generally delivered in the form of a reduction-in-force (RIF) letter. This notice will state the details of the elimination or reduction and will tell you if you have the right to a different position. The reason for the RIF will usually state reorganization due to a number of causes: lack of work, shortage of funds, declining enrollment, library closure, school closure, change of management, or another reason specific to the situation at a particular site.

It is perfectly normal to have a strong reaction on the day of your notice. Take a short time, perhaps a whole day, to feel sorry for yourself. Go ahead and indulge in those activities that will help you deal with the stress: eat, cry, exercise, shop, play bingo, or whatever your coping mechanism may be. Then head to bed and get a good night's sleep because you need to get up early and be ready for a fight.

Contact Your Union

If you pay union dues, you deserve every bit as much help as any other employee. If you are a teacher being replaced by a classified employee, you probably have a grievance. If you are a classified employee being replaced by parent volunteers, you probably have a grievance. Your union will help you to fill out all the correct forms accurately and provide representation during hearings and meetings.

Activate Your Fan Base

Crisis communication, so necessary when programs and staffing are threatened, is a delicate matter. You want to get the message out to as many people as possible, but you don't want to get yourself into trouble at the same time. It is fine to advocate for yourself, but you will be more successful if you get library supporters to do it instead.

- Pass it on.
  Parents and teachers can use their personal and professional networks by writing a brief e-mail message and asking it to be forwarded to all others in their address book. It is a quick and effective way to mobilize other parents for support efforts. One well-written e-mail message can generally be forwarded to most parents within a few days.
- Picketing/demonstrating.
  Check with your union before you take on a project like this. Parents walking in front of the school or district administration building will cause a stir. Having the media present and speakers will make even more of an impression. Will bad press for the school and/or district make a difference in keeping your library open and staffed, or will it alienate your principal and school board? Are you setting yourself up for retribution at a later date? It would be awful to win the battle for your position but lose the respect of your superiors in the process.
- Phone calls.
  A phone tree is an effective way to spread a message and answer questions if you have enough volunteer parents.

- Letter writing/e-mail campaign.
  Especially when it comes down to that very last vote, the school board trustees will be cognizant of the written messages they get from parents. They will typically give more attention and consideration to their decision as parent concerns mount. The key to this is getting a large number of supporters to take the time to write. Sample letters are included later in this chapter.

Mobilization

Can you find 25 people to promote your cause when you kick into crisis mode? Imagine that you reach out to different stakeholders: parents, teachers, principals, students, and other staff members. If you can find 25 promoters, you need to also tap into at least 25 reasons that the library is important. Many will say they are willing to do something, but what? What should they say? Here is a starting list of ideas:

- The library is an important part of the school and has a prominent role in teaching students to love reading and lifelong learning.
- The library provides reading materials to underprivileged students, which helps close the achievement gap that exists due to children growing up in environments void of print.
- The assets in the library are too valuable to sit unused or underused by students and teachers.
- Students benefit from a school librarian's specialized training in developing a collection that supports the curriculum and recreational reading goals. Students can create posters or write letters about how they use the library and why it is important to their academic success.
- Decision-makers would not be happy if it was their loved ones being deprived. Would they allow their children or grandchildren to attend a school with no library?
- Teachers who use the expertise of the school librarian and library resources in their professional practice can share the importance of these in the creation of exceptional lessons/units.
- Teachers count on the school librarian to provide staff development when they need to learn something new, especially with technology and media.
- Teachers are experts within their content area, but school librarians are experts at teaching research and information literacy.
- School librarians know the curriculum being covered at all levels and in all subjects and can help teachers understand what those in their classes have covered in their earlier education and what they will be expected to achieve as they move to a new level.
- Teachers cannot afford to add all the books and resources they need to their classroom, but they share this wish list with the school librarian and resources can be shared with the whole school.
- Students and teachers need the specialized knowledge of the school librarian to overcome stumbling blocks when using the catalog to search for resources.
- School librarians are the experts that know good literature, keep current with new materials, and match students to the book they want or need.

- School librarians help students learn how to use the library and engage in the resource process that is foundational for student success in high school and college.
- Students are invested in the library and can tell the ways that they are involved.
- Students need the availability of the school librarian to help them one-on-one or in small groups.
- Students must be exposed to subscription databases and the peculiarities in their use, and this can only happen through the consolidated budget of the library and the expertise of the teacher-librarian through guided practice.
- Students value the experiences they have that are designed by professional librarians in collaboration with teachers.
- Students value the library environment as the place on campus where they are safe to study, read, and learn.
- Students living in poverty deserve the same quality library programs as children of the wealthy.
- Students benefit from the school librarian's knowledge of the curriculum, standards, teaching methods, and objectives of the teachers.
- Students need school librarians to guide them in finding and processing the overwhelming amount of information, in terms of reliability, validity, authority, appropriateness, and bias.
- Students have to learn twenty-first-century research and information skills to compete in the nation and the world.
- Students benefit from learning to use the information they find ethically and accurately to solve real-world problems with creativity and hard work.
- No Child Left Behind requires that standards be taught and tested. Depending on the state, information-literacy standards may stand alone or be embedded in other content-area standards, but having instruction from a school librarian enhances student performance on such assessments.
- Students must become lifelong learners if they are going to function well in a democracy where they must make careful decisions before they elect the representatives who will govern them.

The 25 talking points listed above are just starters, and you have more that can be added that are particular to your situation. The important point to remember is that advocacy when you are in crisis is different than ongoing advocacy. When you are in crisis, numbers matter. Getting more people from a variety of stakeholders to speak on your behalf is your key to success. Having many different reasons from a variety of points of view will count more than having everyone stand up and say the same thing.

Planning for the Short-Term Battle

Notify your state and national library and school library organizations of the threat to your position or the library program. Check chapter 2 for details about your state. These organizations may have special materials available to help you during this difficult time.

Have a meeting with stakeholders willing to advocate for you. Do this "off-the-clock" and off-campus. Bring information that will help them to focus their efforts. Let them know who is responsible for the decision to make the cuts and why the decision has been made. Let them know the time line of events that will happen before a final decision is made. Remind your supporters that the decision is not personal and that they should not make it about you, but about what the library offers to teachers and students.

Keep the acrimony to a minimum because your supporters may trigger an adversarial situation if they behave angrily. If principals and school board members perceive they are being attacked, they are likely to become defensive. Optimally, they are approached in a peaceful, constructive way so that they are more likely to use library supporter's input to inform their further actions. At the same time, you want supporters to be specific about what they are asking the decision-makers to do. A vague message about how important the school library is in the education of students may end up saving very little and much less than what is needed. For example:

- Instead of reassigning all the school librarians to classroom positions, we will retain one school librarian to split time between three schools.
- Instead of having the libraries closed for half the day, we will have the library open all day on an every other week schedule.
- Instead of closing the library altogether, volunteers are allowed to continue library services as practical.

In each of these cases, your supporters may get the feeling that they've accomplished something, and the trustees will save political face. The reality of these solutions will be that library services are marginalized. Supporters must articulate exactly what they want as an outcome and point out that lesser cuts will be no less devastating.

Beyond letting your supporters know the details of your situation, it is best that your role is one of an advisory nature. You should gather data about your school library program that will help the group to spread the message; standards that are taught, number of items circulated, hours open, number of computers, test scores, and the like. You can also provide study findings, especially from your own state, to the group. Start with Scholastic's "School Libraries Work!," which is packed with pertinent information and study summaries.[2] You will also be able to pass on information about things that may not be readily visible at your library: services to students with disabilities, partnerships with other entities, or special projects and programs.

Encourage someone else to step forward to be the leader of this crisis-advocacy group. This person can delegate tasks, run meetings, and be the official spokesperson for the group. If you have an advisory group for your school library, your leader may be in that group. You will also need a communications director who is responsible for keeping everyone informed and mobilizing all involved when there are important events or meetings.

Make sure that you have as many different kinds of stakeholders as possible. Each stakeholder can be asked to contact groups or individuals. You will want to have library supporters describe in their own words how the school library is important to their students and to them. Make sure you have representation from the students, the parents, and the teachers.

Reach out beyond the school population, too, to the neighborhood at large. Are there schools that feed into your school or district? Where will the students attend next? Are there other groups in the community that have a stake in making sure students are well prepared for the twenty-first century? Find alumni willing to come back and share how the school library made them more successful in higher education or obtaining a good job.

Examine the mission, vision, and goals of the school and/or district and give explicit evidence of where the library supports them. If the school is struggling in a specific area, does it make sense to cut the library program in light of this problem?

Speaking at Meetings

You or your appointed representative should be prepared to speak in support of the school library at any number of meetings beginning with the local school board. Other groups such as service organizations in the community should be offered an opportunity to hear your message.

Boards of Education

The public has the right to address the board on both agenda items and general matters concerning education during the meeting. Generally speakers will be asked to fill out a speaker slip or card before they speak, and it will ask the topic of concern. The board may ask speakers to appear in the order that the cards are turned in, but if there are several distinct topics to discuss, they may group speakers in that way. A time limit may be set for speakers, varying perhaps between two and five minutes. The board may also set a maximum amount of time for any one issue. For this reason, speakers want to be prepared before they fill out a slip.

Community/Public Forums

When major decisions are being made, such as closing libraries or schools, there may be meetings held at the school to let parents and community members speak their minds and air concerns outside of the constraints of a board-meeting environment. The number of participants and their comments at these meetings are very important when influencing further action. If you cannot get a large and vocal group to a meeting such as this, you have little chance of changing the hearts and minds of the decision-makers.

Your advocacy groups should initiate a letter-writing campaign. A sample letter is shown below:

To a superior or school board member:

Dear _____,

It is with deep sadness that I write this letter because I was informed that school librarians are slated for elimination for the upcoming school year. I urge you to reconsider this decision in light of the importance of the library to the academic success of every student. The library is the vital heart of the school, providing access to books, technology, research assistance, and real-world lifelong learning. If we want our students to be successful not only on tests, but also in life, then they need a library that is open during the instructional hours of every school day with a school librarian and support staff to help them find the resources they need to be successful learners.

This district has a reputation for an exceptional school library program, and you have been an important library advocate. Together, teachers and school librarians make sure that every student can be successful because they have learned to use the biggest classroom in the school with its access to a world of information.

I realize that the district is facing a dreadful reduction in funding, but that is why the school library is more important than ever before. The library is where we house the shared resources, allowing greater access to the valuable collection and special teaching expertise that I can offer the entire school.

Our library has # books, # computers, # database subscriptions ... worth more than $xxx,xxx! Only by keeping the library doors open and properly staffed can these resources be available to further student success.

Respectfully,

To a person willing to serve on the library advocacy crisis committee:

Dear _____,

I am writing to you as a fellow parent of a student at _____ School. I am a school volunteer and serve on the library advisory committee. I am very concerned about the recent decision to _____. As a voter, a taxpayer, and a concerned citizen, I understand that the schools need to spend their budgets wisely. With this in mind, it makes no sense to _____ when this is essential to student learning and success.

I am asking you to come learn more about this situation and to serve on a committee of concerned teachers, students, and parents to save this important resource. Your voice is needed!

Time:
Location:

Parents, teachers, and students are invited to this meeting. Collectively, we can communicate the importance of a strong library program in our school—it is essential to our students' success today and in the future.

Please attend this meeting and get involved.

Feel free to contact me at _____ for more information.

Respectfully,

Getting a notice of elimination or reduction requires an appropriate reaction. Communicate with decision-makers and influential people. Gather your library supporters together to form a campaign on behalf of saving the library program. Arm supporters with information that will help them carry the message. Stay positive, keep doing the best job possible, and let your fan base speak on your behalf.

Notes

1. Urban Dictionary, http://www.urbandictionary.com. Retrieved January 18, 2010.

2. "School Libraries Work!" is a free download from Scholastic, Inc., at http://www2.scholastic.com/content/collateral_resources/pdf/s/slw3_2008.pdf.

CHAPTER 10

DeACTivation

School administrators with loss of funding often have to make tough decisions, including trimming staff while finding ways to maintain their programs. This usually translates into reducing the hours of an employee or being given additional duties. When this happens, you have some choices to make.

Ten "DeACTivation" Action Items for School Librarians Who Have Been Given Additional Duties or Who Have Been Reduced in Hours

Do:

✓ Consult with your administrator on priorities to keep your relationship positive and professional
✓ Continue to do your job to the best of your ability during the hours you are paid, but do not put in extra time for free
✓ Post new hours and policies so that patrons are prepared for the changes
✓ Delegate library tasks to volunteers and student helpers that do not require your expertise and focus on those things that only you can do
✓ Restructure the use of the library so that nonacademic or nonproductive activities aren't competing with legitimate users
✓ If the library schedule is completely impacted, shift your hours so that you can have open access to the library before or after school
✓ Talk to others in the same situation and share best practices
✓ Simplify and automate tasks that are slowing you down
✓ If something absolutely, positively must be finished and you don't have time to do it, ask for help or additional hours
✓ Find something new or different to enhance your program without requiring extensive time and planning

Our definitions:

deactivation

1. Discontinuation of activities. *It is physically impossible to do a good job when hours are cut unless priorities are set and deactivation of less important tasks occurs.*
2. Reassignment of effort to protect yourself from overwork. *The school librarian let the repair pile grow (deactivation) in order to continue providing instruction to students.*

Deactivation Quiz

Read through each of the 30 common library tasks and then categorize them. Use a pencil since you can only put 5 tasks in each category.

- Adding materials to the **catalog**.
- **Advocacy**.
- Arranging for **special events**—book fairs, author visits, and field trips.
- **Assisting students** with research and projects.
- **Assisting teachers** with acquiring resource materials.
- Attending school **meetings**.
- Changing **displays** and bulletin boards
- Chasing **overdue** materials.
- **Circulating** books and materials.
- **Cleaning**, straightening, tidying—the library must remain safe and useable.
- **Collaborating** and co-teaching with classroom teachers.
- **Collection development** and maintenance—should weeding be pushed to the back burner? Can you give repair tasks to others?
- **Communications**—will the weekly newsletter become quarterly or cease to exist?
- Creating **instructional materials** with teacher.
- **Developing readers**—Story times and book talks.
- **Encouraging** lifelong learning.
- **Instructing** visiting **classes**.
- Maintaining audiovisual **equipment** and computers.
- **Planning**.
- Professional **reading** and development—will you be able to keep up with current trends and material reviews?
- Providing **staff development** for others—will you provide staff development for teachers, classified staff, parents, or administrators?
- **Shelving**—could you live with books grouped by author and not necessarily also alphabetized by title?
- **Supervision** of student helpers and managing student behavior.

Must be done by me	Should be done by me	Nice if it was done by me

Could be done by paraprofessional or volunteer	Task supported by district staff	Not my job or something I can give up

- **Technical** duties—maintaining the Web site and administrating network programs like Accelerated Reader or Reading Counts.
- **Textbook distribution**—very few schools outside of California require the librarian to take care of the textbooks, but the Williams Settlement is specific that every student must have textbooks within a prescribed period of time.

Quiz results:

1. Go back and put a star by each one that *directly* influences student achievement. How student-focused were you?
2. Were you able to fit everything you *must do* in that category? Are some *must do* activities in the *should do* category because you ran out of spaces?
3. Will you complete all your *must do* and *should do* tasks before you begin *nice to do* ones?
4. Which tasks were you willing to sacrifice to volunteers or give up altogether?

School librarians may have some warning that the situation is going to change the next semester or the next school year. These warnings are often retracted, and things remain the same. On the other hand, the reduction may hold. It is also possible that reductions happen just as the school year is beginning or even into a semester. What happens next is up to the flexibility of the school librarian.

Assessing the New Situation

Despite your best efforts, and those of your library supporters, the library program is going to be affected in the immediate future. Every situation is different, but it is likely you will be faced by one of the situations below.

Library Closed

In the most unfortunate of events, the library is closed. Teacher-librarians may be assigned to a classroom of elementary students or a subject specialty when they have the proper credentials and seniority. Removing staffing from a library is a difficult situation because union contracts and education codes may dictate that the library must be secured and locked if no one is available to manage the program.

If there aren't legal reasons against allowing the room to remain available, the administrator might think the facility can be run by parent volunteers. In some states, it is illegal to use a volunteer to replace a paid position. A next step is to ask classroom teachers to handle circulation themselves when they bring their students to the library. This is seldom successful since they may not understand the circulation system, might not realize when students have forgotten their books, and won't have time to put returned materials back on the shelves correctly or to put away other materials.

Even if the doors are locked and everyone is told to stay out, teachers will want to continue to use the resources inside. Students and teachers will find reasons to pilfer materials, and the catalog will quickly be irrelevant. The administration may decide to divide the collection and distribute everything to the classrooms. In either scenario, the valuable contents of the library will be marginalized, lost, or sit dormant.

If this is the situation at your school and you think you will return next year, you need to talk to the principal about the options for the library and what can be done to minimize the damage to the collection and to the program. It might be wise to plan to visit the building and the library once a month during the year to see if the library is being taken care of as planned.

Library Staff Eliminations

Personnel are usually the greater part of any school district budget. To eliminate or reduce positions or even to replace a position with a less qualified and therefore less expensive person is one way to balance budgets. Such plans will mean either fewer hours assigned to one building or someone to manage a program without the requisite education to do the job.

A school librarian may lose clerical support. This means that all clerical duties are returned to the profession and suddenly there is less time to collaborate or to teach. A period of adjustment will be needed to reschedule in the new situation.

The library may be open during the school day for the same period of time as before, but with a paraprofessional expected to run it without supervision. When a school librarian's position is eliminated, both educational and technical aspects of the job may be impossible for the paraprofessional, who usually has little formal training.

The district may try to cut costs by eliminating professional school librarians at the sites and centralizing services at the district level. When this happens, collection development no longer reflects the needs of the school. Additionally, the intimate knowledge of special materials in the existing collection and the expertise in their applications is lost.

Additional Duties

The school librarian may be given additional duties that are outside the assignments to the library such as overseeing textbook distribution, serving as testing coordinator, or being the administrative alternate when the principal is off-campus. Perhaps the library is going to serve as the in-school suspension room, study hall, or holding spot for students who cannot participate in physical education. Supervising students quickly becomes a drain on the ability to work with individual students on their projects or teaching research methods and certainly does not allow time to collaborate with teachers. School librarians may be assigned to teach classes, either in the library or another classroom. This could be related to the library, such as a research-methods course, or it could be a regular section of another subject that the librarian is qualified to teach, such as an English or history class.

With a growing need for intervention teachers when students are failing courses or scoring well below expected proficiency levels, administrators might look to the school librarian to take on a period or two of tutorials. Even if the school librarian is teaching only for an hour or two a day, the school librarian will need prep time, further taking away time devoted to library service.

Split Assignments

As budgets are decreased so that students and teachers are perceived to have a professional overseeing their programs, school librarians may be responsible for running two or more libraries. Often this is with the help of paraprofessionals, but the challenge is to split time equitably between schools. The distribution of time may be based on the number of students in a school so that a larger school might have the librarian for four days and another school only one. This may mean alternating weeks or days between sites or traveling within the same school day. It will be difficult to keep connected to the daily happenings and needs at multiple schools, and collaboration becomes less and less effective. Library instruction can become sporadic and disjointed and may be seldom taught when students need to learn research skills. Students and teachers may become frustrated with projects that cannot be finished because no one is available as a resource at the time it is needed.

Reduction of Hours or Days

The school library may be open fewer hours than the instructional day. Students may have the chance to visit the library only if their teacher brings them for a scheduled activity. Additionally, teachers will have difficulty consulting with the school librarian or gathering resources because the school librarian is actively instructing students during the entire time the library is open. Teachers who cannot gain access either before or after school because the library is closed will simply stop using it except when they come in with their students.

As explained earlier, when the library is closed, it must be secured as well. One difficulty will be maintaining the collection if it is in an open area that cannot be locked or otherwise protected. When the library is staffed only for a portion of the day or on certain days of the week, the materials and computers can become targets for misuse and theft. Even well-intentioned "borrowers" will forget to return items, and the collection will be compromised.

Bottom Line

Making the best of the situation is important because a time may come when positions and library programs are considered for reinstatement. It is tempting to let everyone feel the sting of needing some assistance or material and not being able to have it because of cuts to the program. Ultimately, however, this further jeopardizes the role and the ability of school librarians to recover their former status should that opportunity present itself.

It may be a challenge. When library services are cut or eliminated, patrons become accustomed to finding what they need elsewhere, and therefore they become less likely to believe they need these services from the school library. It is true that it is important for the reduction of services to be felt, but unless others speak up for returning school librarians to the library so that they can continue to provide exceptional service, this won't happen.

Even though school librarians cannot meet the needs of students and teachers when the library is closed, they can make the open hours as productive and valuable as possible. Then they focus efforts on building a strong school library virtual presence to pick up the slack when they are unavailable. Building a portal that encourages students and teachers to use the library's resources, even when it is not physically open, keeps the school library as their primary information source. This requires building a Web site with links to needed information. Databases can be open to students and teachers and how to make effective use of them can be taught when the professional is on site. If the school librarian is at another school, it may be possible to consult e-mail to answer any critical questions almost as if they were on site. This can help alleviate some of the loss.

Meeting Your Administrator to Set Priorities and Policies

When this is happening to you, review your answers to the quiz at the beginning of this chapter and add other tasks that must be or should be done. Take your list of responsibilities with you when you meet with your administrator so that you don't forget anything. This will probably prove eye-opening for anyone who is a decision-maker and who may not have thought about all the responsibilities that must be juggled. Principals may have a high learning curve because most are unaware of what it really takes to manage a school library and program. Explaining the time it takes to carry out duties can also be eye-opening. If the perception is that the greatest use is circulation of materials, it is still necessary to show the number of items being checked out and how long that process takes and how long it takes to have materials returned and replaced on shelves. However, that cannot be used as either the primary role or the most time-consuming. The length of time it takes to work to prepare for teaching students, collaborating with teachers, and implementing new units of instruction are also time measurements you should collect.

Inevitably, you will be asked to add, move to a different priority, or delete items from the list. Seek consensus on the prioritization of all activities. Once you are in agreement about the priorities, look realistically at what has been set for you. Be clear and up front about those items that will absolutely be done, those that will probably be done, and those that can't or probably won't get done. It is hard to give up favorite projects or tasks, but not everything can be done when you have less time. This is a good time to ask what should be considered a triggering event that requires you to meet or communicate further with your administrator. Don't forget to discuss your schedule, hours of operation, circulation policies that may need to be changed, and tasks that you will no longer be doing.

Create a Stop-Doing List

Examine all the commonplace activities that take most of your time and see if they can be streamlined or eliminated. This includes mundane things like circulating materials; train a helper for each class or have students do it themselves. Have overdue lists e-mailed to teachers or students instead of printing and delivering them. Reduce shelving time by putting frequently circulated items on a "Favorites" shelf or allow students to choose items directly from the book cart. Find a helper to turn on all the computers in the morning and another to turn them all off at the end of the day.

Even if you can't completely stop offering certain services, you can stop being the one who has to do it. For example, many school librarians find themselves spending an inordinate amount of time making copies for teachers and monitoring copies made by students. Sometimes the process is to collect money from students, and that takes more time. Again, a trained helper can oversee this process for students, and teachers can make their own copies. Or perhaps you can have the copy machine moved to another area of the building.

Students can be trained, usually with gentle reminders, to tidy up after themselves, straighten the shelves if they see books falling over, return items to carts, and push in chairs. The time spent keeping students accountable for the condition of their school library before they leave is time saved for you to do more important work after they go.

Stop doing things for teachers that they could and should do for themselves. For example, do you run reports for some teachers because they are uncomfortable doing it? Do you update their assignments on the school Web page simply because you were the one who set it up in the first place? All of these examples are things where it is more appropriate for you to serve as a coach to show others how to do it rather than continue to use your time doing it indefinitely. Collaborating with teachers is critical, and this is not a place to skimp. Still, you may have some projects that teachers are now ready to continue without any help from you. Ask yourself if you're spending time on the tried and true at the expense of doing something bold and new.

Consider Changes in Policy and Communicate Those Changes

Mitigate reductions to services by changing policies. For example, if classes will be visiting every other week rather than weekly, you could encourage them to check out more books when they do come and extend the checkout periods. If you let them have a six-week loan period, remind them that they would need to return any book someone else has requested.

Create multiple ways for patrons to communicate with you when you're not on site: e-mail, voice mail, bulletin boards, mailboxes, or request clipboards. When you get into work, you can take these requests, prioritize them, and work your way through them. If having face-to-face meetings with collaborating teachers becomes difficult to impossible, create an easy way for them to communicate much of the planning information through an online or paper form. Encourage teachers to schedule planning visits further in advance to give you time to prepare.

Provide a school library update whenever possible. This is an important part of letting everyone know what has changed. This is your chance to let everyone know when you are available to help them and to provide access. This can be done with teachers at the first staff meeting and then reminding them again when you talk with students on their first visit to the library. Communicate with families, too, with a note home to parents as a reminder if students will be bringing home materials less often.

Once a decision is in place, support the decision-makers as much as possible because it is being "advertised" as a balanced-budget necessity and the community will agree. Whining about it constantly will achieve nothing. You must build your case for when the next budget is being developed. When your library schedule does not allow for another teacher's afternoon class visits because you are teaching a class or you are at another school and the library is closed in the afternoons, there is nothing you can do to satisfy the teacher who needs to use the library specifically at that time. When the teacher complains to you, you can remind him or her of the importance of the library in the education of students, something they can help you demonstrate to decision-makers. Then see what you can do to help the teacher through electronic communication or a scheduled time when you are available.

Another solution is to offer to go with the teacher to try to figure something out with the help of the principal. This opens the door for a discussion about how to accommodate teachers who are denied the resources they need. It may be possible to send a collection or print materials to the classroom and a list of your appropriate databases for those who have access to the Internet. Be firm that the teacher not be given free access to the library in your absence, but remain open to creative solutions. Be careful not to be seen as a troublemaker who is encouraging teachers to complain about the lack of access to the library. It is one thing to respond appropriately to a teacher concern and quite another to constantly be stirring the pot of discontent.

Maintain a Positive Attitude

Although you are being asked to do more with less, a welcoming and helpful persona is crucial to maintaining the reputation of the library as the heart of the school. Remember that you are there first and foremost to be a resource for your patrons to help teachers teach and students learn. Teachers will realize that you can't do everything you used to do, and they will generally be helpful and sympathetic. Cynical or sarcastic library workers can become toxic, doing more damage to their cause. This can be seen when they start every statement with, "My hours were cut ... " or, "I have no help so...." When you are asked to do something that you just can't do because of the constraints you are working within, this is the time to approach your administrator for help. It is one thing to say no yourself, and quite another when the no comes from the principal.

Bad experiences in your school library at any time can permanently disengage patrons from using and valuing all libraries and your library in particular. It is extremely critical when teachers may be given more students to teach with fewer resources and they may even get a pay raise only if they can raise test scores in their classroom. The obviously constantly overwhelmed school librarian will find teachers avoiding the school librarian for assistance if they perceive that they are adding to an already intolerable workload. Teachers will get frustrated when they have a desperate need and the school librarian does not seem to have any time to help. They may even begin to believe that it is better to have no library at all than one where they are supposed to get help but don't. Giving teachers a time when you can help them is essential. This could mean juggling your priorities yet one more time, but the perception will be that help is available, although maybe not immediately.

Students will feel unwelcome if school librarians give the impression that they don't have time to help with their requests. A drop in the numbers of students who use the library is an indication that they are finding other ways to satisfy their information and reading material needs.

Administrators will be fully aware of how students and teachers are being treated badly because negative experiences tend to be shared more often than positive ones. When it comes time to reinstate library services, it may not be seen as a good use of money because no one uses or values it any longer. With reinstatement of funding in schools, administrators will evaluate the programs they have and decide which ones are the best investments to enhance academic achievement. When funding becomes available, principals sensing the negativity of the school librarian may divert money to the technology department to start an information lab or to the reading-resource program to hire reading specialists.

Give Up Perfectionism for Your Health

School librarians who are working to the best of their ability may have stress and borderline burnout because they cannot cope with failing to reach standards they've set for themselves. Stress is caused by working too much or too hard, not being able to manage own time, or feeling that something or everything is out of control. It is not surprising that school librarians feel stress when they can no longer provide the high level of service or even a service that was offered in the past. Prolonged periods of stress can bring on illness and depression. It is important to set realistic objectives for new situations rather than trying and failing to keep the same services that were in place when more staff, more budget, and more hours were available.

One way to cope with this problem is to find other school librarians who are going through a similar situation. This support network will be invaluable as you discover solutions to similar problems and shortcuts to getting things done. Sharing bibliographies and ideas for units of instruction can help improve instruction without starting from the beginning.

Instead of lying awake in bed thinking of all the things you have to do, start keeping a list of projects that you will begin when you can. Putting it down on paper releases it from the immediate need to obsess over something you can't act upon to something you will do in the future. Looking at everything on a list can also help you to prioritize your projects. Have you been waiting to do something that actually won't take much time because there is a huge project that you feel has precedence? It may be better to take a break from overwhelming tasks to check a few easy-to-do items off your list and rejuvenate yourself with those successes.

Provide Value by Maintaining a Student Focus

Keeping student learning as the central focus of your activities sounds easy, but in fact it is far from simple. The complex interaction of tasks required to run a school library has many facets that don't seem to directly influence student learning. For example, shelving books, repairing torn covers and pages, and cataloging are necessary activities in most school libraries, but these do not in and of themselves affect student learning. These activities must occur for the library to serve as a resource for the students and teachers:

- If the books aren't shelved properly, the patrons will not be able to find them.
- If books aren't repaired, they may fall apart.
- If the books aren't cataloged, students and teachers won't find the correct resources when they search the catalog.

However, students may be able to help reshelve books, or a group of students doing service learning might be able to help. If books are in bad shape, they might be collected and sent to a bookbinder. When they return, they will be much more attractive than those repaired in house. If parent volunteers want to repair books, they might be taught how to do this. Finally, books should be purchased from a jobber who provides cataloging, preferably in electronic format that matches your online public access catalog.

Activities that yield high benefits to teachers and students include taking time to provide alternate paths for various levels of differentiation (English learners, high achievers, or reluctant learners). This is directly related to student achievement. Running a literature club encourages reading of good, quality titles and discussion that enhances students' comprehension and critical-thinking skills.

When you approach your principal about needing additional time to complete tasks that directly relate to student learning, you may be surprised at the creative ways that can be found to carve a niche for this. The principal might be able to watch students taking their exams so that you can continue collaborative planning as previously arranged with a teacher. You might ask to be excused from a nonlibrary duty such as overseeing students as they get on buses in order to work with a group of teachers planning a cooperative unit across grade levels or subject levels.

Maintain and Grow Your Fan Base

It is more important than ever that you cultivate school library friends who will speak about the impact of the cuts and also about the good things you are continuing to do in the library. You don't want to be the target of future reductions, and you want to keep the library in line for reinstatement just as soon as possible.

The people who stood by your side and fought for the library program will be discouraged that the reductions happened in spite of their efforts. Tell them how important their continued support remains, and let them know that although cuts occurred, they may have been less drastic because of their activities. Also tell them that their involvement planted the seeds that still need to be watered in order for the library to be restored to its former status.

Use Technology to Simplify

New ways of sharing information and collaborating electronically can help you free up time, as well. If you can make a presentation for students to view when you aren't there, it can be useful for more than one class. Helping teachers be prepared to give answers to probable questions further instructs them about library holdings and databases. You could also have students e-mail questions to you, especially if you could be online even though you are in a different location.

Use wikis to share lesson plans, projects, and ideas with others. Create an online reservation system for teachers to schedule their class visits with an easy way for them to indicate what they will need from you during this time. Build your collection-development wish lists on publisher sites developed specifically for that purpose. Then, if money is suddenly available, you simply return and print the list. Instead of driving across town for a meeting with a small group, try using teleconferencing technology that allows you to attend from your office.

Keep Connected

When you become overwhelmed at work, it seems more difficult to also stay involved in your local librarians' group and other groups in your area as well as your professional organizations. These activities are more important than ever, however, because they can connect you to resources and timesavers that you wouldn't discover otherwise. You will find others there dealing with the same issues that you face. You can also tap into the advocacy efforts of others to find out what is working and what isn't. Should your position be taken by someone with more seniority and you are jobless, you will need these contacts to provide you with news of openings in their district. Having a personal reference from someone you know may be the very thing that nets you a career opportunity elsewhere.

Make Wish Lists and Be Ready for Reinstatement

When your program is reinstated, it may be that special funds will be found or created for the purpose of library programs. A conversation about what you would do with extra funding, extra staff, or increased hours should not leave you unprepared. Be ready to share what activities have been suspended and how they could be resumed. Additionally, have new ideas to share about programs or projects that have come to your attention but haven't had a chance to occur.

Look for Alternative Opportunities

If things are looking bleak at your site(s) and there is little hope for reinstatement or relief in the near or distant future, you might begin looking for a change. Be prepared for stiff competition because others may be in a similar situation. However, it is good to be prepared rather than surprised. Start by updating your resume and determining whether you are willing to move out of the area or work in a different kind of library environment.

Most organizations require you to fill out applications online and attach your resume. If the job market is flooded with unemployed teachers and librarians, it may be necessary to fill out dozens of applications before you get a single response of interest. Use your network of library colleagues to find openings and ask them to recommend you. Practice your interview skills if it has been a long time since you were job hunting.

Check the job listings on various sites:

SchoolSpring—a nationwide database of job opportunities in education, http://www.schoolspring.com/find/librarian_jobs.cfm

LISjobs.com, http://www.lisjobs.com/. This resource is specific to library openings nationwide and lists school, public, academic, and special library openings.

The American Library Association and your local associations may have listings of openings as well.

Moving Up and Out

Is it time to shake up things by doing something else? Perhaps this is just the encouragement you need to return to school to get that higher degree. If you have the funding and support, you might just add a new teaching area to your present credential. Have you considered getting your administrative credential to open management possibilities within your district or pursuing opportunities with another district?

Responding appropriately to a reduction or elimination to the school library program requires a change in focus. Redesigning services is the first step to deactivating, or redefining, the scope of what can be accomplished. Meet with your administrator to set priorities and ask for their help in communicating to others the change that is occurring. Keep a positive attitude and work smarter instead of harder by incorporating technology and giving up on perfection. Your student-leaning focused services will help you retain and grow your fan base and provide value to the whole school. Maintain your membership and participation in professional associations, or determine if this is the time for a change in your career path.

CHAPTER 11

The RetroACTive Librarian

As situations improve, school librarians are reinstated and they return to a library that has been closed or perhaps managed by someone who was not a professional librarian. This presents challenges when the situation is a familiar one. It presents an even greater challenge if the return is to a different library situation. Each situation requires a careful analysis of what is found there. It begins with looking everywhere for everything. It may be that the substitute has left new materials in boxes in closets because of uncertainty in what to do with them.

Ten "ReACTivation" Action Items for School Librarians Who Return to a Library That Has Been Closed

Do:

✓ Check everywhere for library materials and equipment that may be stored in the library or elsewhere
✓ Make sure everything is cleaned thoroughly for safety reasons as well as to restore the beauty of the library
✓ When time allows, conduct an inventory to ascertain which items were pilfered or damaged during the time it was closed and need to be replaced immediately
✓ Weed out books in the collection that are outdated, superceded, or inappropriate, and begin filling the gaps that have occurred during the period the library had no collection budget or was closed
✓ As quickly as possible, throw a grand reopening celebration and invite everyone but especially the decision-makers and the supporters that helped get the library program reinstated
✓ Welcome teachers and students back into the library announcing new programs, services, and materials

✓ Bring classes in for orientation—many if not most students may have forgotten how to use the library (or if no professional was in charge for a longer period of time, students may have never learned)
✓ Begin the collaboration process immediately by asking teachers about their research papers and projects so you can be prepared to assist students
✓ Create a school library advisory group with members chosen from teachers, students, and parents
✓ Update technology as a first priority

Our definitions:

reactivation

1. Resumption of school library activities. *The reactivation of the school library as the hub of the school was a cause for jubilation.*
2. Beginning again. *The school librarian realized that the reactivation of the library program was similar to what a library might need when recovering from a natural disaster.*

Quiz: Matching—Pick the Best Answer

_____ 1. The ideal library environment should be
_____ 2. The most important quality for a school librarian
_____ 3. The reason that students come is because the library is
_____ 4. Teachers sign up for a visit because the library is
_____ 5. Advertise that the library is
_____ 6. My schedule is
_____ 7. I shouldn't forget
_____ 8. I strive to be
_____ 9. I have a _____ for this library
_____ 10. I will know the library is successful when it is

A. a mentor	I. impacting student learning	Q. to get materials into students' hands
B. a leader	J. mission	R. to learn
C. buzzing with activity	K. neat and tidy	S. to relax
D. enjoyable	L. objective	T. to teach
E. exceptional service	M. open	U. to thank others
F. flexible	N. organized	V. vision
G. full of amazing resources	O. quiet	
H. goal	P. the heart of the school	

Quiz results:

1. Possible answers: C, D, F, G, I, K, M, N, O
2. Possible answers: F, G, K, N, O
3. Possible answers: C, D, G, M, N, O, P

4. Possible answers: C, D, G, I, M, N, O, P
5. Possible answers: C, D, F, G, I, K, M, N, O, P
6. Possible answers: C, D, F, I, M
7. Possible answers: Q, R, S, T, U
8. Possible answers: A, B, G, K, N
9. Possible answers: H, J, L, V
10. Possible answers: C, D, G, I, K, M, N, P

Your advocacy efforts paid off in a big way. The library that was closed has been given another chance. Everyone is excited about it, but what must be done before you can open the doors and welcome everyone back in?

You will find a list of considerations below. As you go through them, remember that you will need to make a list of those items, resources, equipment, and furnishings that must be replaced. You will then need to estimate the cost of replacing them, establish a priority of how the needs should be fulfilled, and make an appointment as quickly as possible with your principal. Recognizing that an economic situation has probably not changed for the better, you need to use care in establishing the list and justifying each proposed need or purchase with why it is essential. Remember also that principals are not always knowledgeable in what is needed in a school library, especially if their perception is that it is a place to get books. Your presentation of your prioritized list of needs provides you with an opportunity to, one more time, explain the library and its role in the lives of students and teachers.

If at all possible, bring the principal to the school library. Make sure you have established enough time. Having the principal in the library allows you to show and tell by pointing out dangerous furnishings, old computers, and outdated materials or those in poor condition. You should have coffee or tea and cookies to establish a more relaxed atmosphere. Be sure to have some good things to report as well as the list of disasters, and be sure to say thank you at the end.

Safety

Check library furnishings and equipment to be sure they are still safe to use. Depending on the length of closure, pests may have infested areas of the library. A thorough cleaning will remove not only dust, but any animal droppings as well. Check all the power cords to make sure they haven't been gnawed, and go through every drawer and closet. Look for water damage and mold.

Inventory, Weeding, and Cataloging

Make a call to everyone in the school for the return of library materials. If teachers (or students if the closure was a brief period) have borrowed or been given items from the library during the closure, ask them to be returned so you can make a full accounting. If you are lucky, the books are still in the catalog and your circulation system is still functioning.

The worst-case scenario is your being assigned to a school library that has no catalog and no bar codes or other identifying mechanism. You may want to start with the old-fashioned pockets and cards so that you can begin circulating materials quickly.

When you have no catalog, your first purchase should be a library software system, preferably Web-based, so that you can begin building your online public access catalog. This is a major project that will take much time and effort to implement, but it is necessary for having an efficient, modern library that prepares students for twenty-first-century learning. You will have additional costs to consider: bar codes, bar code scanners, and other peripherals as needed by the specific system that is used.

Complications may occur if the circulation system and catalog that was used previously is no longer working or wasn't saved in a format that can be used in newer systems. Work with your information systems/information technology experts at your school district to recover data, if at all possible, because it will save you a tremendous amount of time and effort. At a minimum, it would be nice to have a shelf list that showed what was in the library at the time it was closed.

If the catalog has not been updated, you will need to determine the best way to get holdings into the catalog while your program is up and running. Trying to have everything perfect before you open the library means a delayed reopening. Better public relations come with opening and putting collection management aside.

If time allows, you must do a thorough inventory. See if you can enlist student volunteer help with this so that it is accomplished while you are doing other things. After the inventory has been completed, be sure to mark everything missing as lost or simply delete the records from the system. Logic will tell you there is little possibility that items will be recovered.

If the library has been closed for a significant time, it may be that you can open using a card catalog with cards and pockets in the books. At least you will have a place to start and can get opened quickly. Check to find out if the rest of the schools in your district are using an online union catalog or one that you can use with an additional license. Look into the cost of a retrospective conversion, where you contract with an outside company to convert your card catalog to electronic records.

Weed out the books that have become outdated or damaged during the time it has been closed. Examine the reference books closely to see if they are still usable. Have pages been removed?

Filling the Gaps Quickly

One of the problems when you reopen a library is that everything seems old. The newest book in your collection may be a decade old. Students want to have the new, popular titles that their friends are reading or that are on display at the bookstore. Movies and television shows often set off an interest in new books that you probably won't have. Begin as quickly as possible to grow your collection.

1. If you have money, purchase a "starting collection" of books from a major book vendor. These titles may come as a carefully selected number of items, making it easy to get an influx of new items on the shelf.
2. If you have just a little money, hold a book fair to try to raise some funds. Purchasing items at your own book fair generally makes your money go farther, and the books offered by these companies are popular, current titles.
3. If you don't have money, ask for donations. Accept anything in good shape that is appropriate for your school audience. When taking donations, be sure to ask permission to sell titles that can't be used in the library. This may generate a little more money to buy additional titles.

Get Patrons Back into the Library Habit

The structure and grade levels served by your school will determine how and when you can get all the students into the library to get them oriented to its organization, to set rules, and to hopefully get them into the habit of coming often to use it.

- Elementary
  Classes are often on a fixed schedule, visiting on a regular basis as a whole class during that teacher's prep time. If you can ask teachers to remain for the first visit, much of what you will cover will be something they have heard during your presentation at a teachers' meeting and will serve as reinforcement. They can also listen to student questions so they will know what they need to reinforce. If this occurs early in the semester, teachers may not be as reluctant to give up their planning period as they might later when they have papers to grade and revised lessons to plan.

  Students will need to be reminded of correct library behavior, how to use and protect materials, and online database availability. This is followed by a quick tour of the library to see where resources are located. Remind them of where to check out and return materials, the resources available, and the location and use of computers, printers, and copy machines.

  Remind them that the school library is open during non-instructional time, allowing them to visit before school, after school, and at recess or lunch. Tell them the times when they can come individually or in small groups during the school day as well.

- Middle school and high school
  With the reopening or the return of a professional school librarian, it is important that all students get information on library use as quickly as possible and to make sure all students are given the message. You might ask your colleagues for some suggestions. One is offered below.

  Middle and high school students will come to the library with their subject-area teachers, so you need to decide if you are going to try to reach all students with a grade-level approach so that you don't repeat to a student who might come in with the language arts or English teacher one class period and the science teacher the next. Think about taping your orientation and asking teachers to play it during homeroom. If you time the sessions to the length of time teachers are given to take attendance and other bookkeeping tasks, you can probably cover all within one week. Ask students to help you make these so that they both interest the students and are clear to the viewer. It will not allow for questions that may arise, so place your e-mail address at the beginning and the end and ask teachers to post your address in the room either as a paper announcement or on the corner of their white board.

Eat Cake

Your return to your library is a success to celebrate, and it's time to eat cake! Take time to reflect on all the hard work it took to advocate for the reopening of the library. Thank the people who helped you along the way and invite them for cake. Applaud the school board and administrators who made the decisions by inviting them to your reopened library and serve them cake. When they are there, you will be able to show off your reactivated space. Let students conduct tours of the library and the resources now available to them with someone to help them make the best use of them. The students will share their enthusiasm in a way that your visitors will remember. It's the perfect time to invite the media to show the community what has happened in your school. School board members will enjoy having their pictures in the paper or even on television. Your principal will be honored as a leading school administrator. Making a scrapbook of this day may be all the evidence you need when the thought surfaces of reducing school library services or cutting professional staff.

The adage states that you can never go home again, but sometimes you are able to do just that. Depending upon the amount of time you have been away, you will have a great deal to do with what you find. In some cases, the library may have been running smoothly with materials circulating and being returned almost as if you were there. However, students will still need to be retaught and given opportunities to reuse those skills, both searching and critical thinking, that have been missing in your absence.

If the situation has deteriorated, you may have some almost insurmountable odds to overcome. You will need to make a careful analysis of what it will take to return the library to its former state. In a way, this challenge may give you an opportunity to get different resources that have been developed in the time away; different resources will give you the opportunity to help teachers move into a twenty-first-century learning environment. Whatever the challenge, you are just the person to find successful solutions.

Appendix A: Fund-raising

Fund-raising is always a challenge, and in economic downturns, everyone is going after the same pots of gold, so to speak. Before you launch a fund-raising effort, check with those around you to see if you can join in their efforts for a part of their fund-raising event and share a percentage of the profit. This will gain you good will, and they will be more willing to help you with your project.

When you work alone, it is your total responsibility to choose the activity, find the location, get out the publicity, and carry out the project and it would take away valuable time and effort from your "day" job. If others feel you are competing with them, they may boycott your efforts.

When your fund-raising depends upon the students' ability to make donations, you may have many who have limited extra funds. You will need to decide how to let these students participate so that they do not feel like outcasts. If you are having a book sale, try to get an outside agency to provide a "book coupon" for deserving students so they can select a book to take home. It may be the only book the child has ever owned.

Some suggested ways to raise money are shown below. Many are traditional and many are more creative fund-raising ideas to use, but in general they fall into six categories: (1) sales, (2) events, (3) performances, (4) services, (5) games of chance, and (6) donations. Please remember that they will all take a great deal of time and others to help with the planning, gathering prizes, holding the event, and doing the thank-you notes afterward. Assessing this time commitment before you begin will help you decide if such an undertaking is going to be feasible. In some instances, it may be wiser to build a case for better funding from the school board.

Sales

Auctions

Live

Participants bid openly against one another, with each subsequent bid higher than the previous bid. An auctioneer is needed, and it is best to issue numbered paddles to qualified buyers before the event. The auction ends when no participant is willing to bid further, at which point the highest bidder pays the bid.

Luck of the auction

This auction is very similar to the silent auction (described later) except that it adds a raffle component. This is very successful when you have a large number of people, but none that are particularly wealthy. All the items are set out on tables with a clear bowl (such as a fishbowl, punchbowl, or vase) placed next to each item. The bidding on items is done by purchasing tickets and placing them in the bowls for specific items. Participants can buy any number of tickets, which generally have a fairly low cost. At the close of the auction period, the winning ticket for each auction item is then drawn from the corresponding bowl. The more tickets a person deposits in a bowl, the better their chance of winning the item. Highly desirable items will draw a lot of tickets, but people who would never be able to bid several hundred dollars for an item will try their luck with one or two $1 tickets. Lucky winners get a great deal because ticket costs are low compared to the ultimate value of the auction items.

Online

Companies will host online auctions on your behalf (or you can use eBay on your own) when you provide the items. This widens your audience considerably, but there are additional costs involved, such as seller's fees and shipping.

Silent

Instead of using an auctioneer, items are placed on tables and bids are written on a sheet of paper. At the predetermined end of the auction, the highest listed bidder wins the item. Silent auctions allow many items to be offered simultaneously and give participants something to do as they roam the room and keep an eye on their bids.

. . . for a day

This auction may be held in one of two different ways. The first is to offer a specific job "for a day" that someone would like to do. This could be principal for a day, librarian for a day, or teacher for a day. The other way is to recruit others and put them (and yourself) up for auction as a worker for a day. You can hold an auction at school where teachers bid for students, who will then have to help them with all their chores, like filing and tidying the classroom. Alternatively, your teachers can offer themselves up for tasks.

Bake sale

Get as many people as possible to bring homemade baked goods that can be sold to other supporters or the general public. Try to get favorite teachers to bake Mrs. Clapp's Famous Fudge or Principal's Pumpkin Pie. For variety, try a cookie collaborative with at least 20 varieties of cookies. Then charge an entry price of $5, and customers can get up to 10 cookies (one of each kind they'd like to try).

Book fair

Holding a book fair is a good library fund-raiser for several reasons. It promotes the very thing that libraries are all about: books and reading! Librarians can also use working at the book fair as part of the market research that goes into collection development. It is important to know what kids are interested in reading, what parents actually choose for their children, and what teachers want. Many times, teachers will be able to post a wish list and parents can purchase books that the teacher will use in the classroom. You'll also be able to see new titles that the bookseller is promoting. Finally, if you are offered credit toward books instead of cash, you can usually have the books in your hands immediately instead of the usual process of creating a purchase order and waiting for delivery.

Book fairs are available from big and small companies, both nationwide and regional. There are benefits to having a book fair at your site over a longer period and having an "in-store" book fair at a local bookstore.

Barnes and Noble (in-store), http://www.barnesandnoble.com/bookfairs/index.asp

Scholastic, http://www.scholastic.com/bookfairs/

Usborne Books, http://www.usborne-books.com/bookfair.htm

California
  Mrs. Nelson's Book Fairs, http://bookcompany.mrsnelsons.com/index.html

Chicago area
  ABC Fairs, http://www.abcfairs.com/
  Personalized Book Fairs, http://www.personalizedbookfairs.com/

Georgia
  Georgia School Book Fairs, http://www.georgiaschoolbookfairs.com/
  Turtle Express Books, http://www.turtleexpressbooks.com/

New England area
  Book Fairs by Book Ends, http://www.bookfairsbybookends.com/

Texas
  Adventure Land Book Fairs, http://www.adventurelandbookfairs.com

Book sale

Public libraries are able to sell off their old holdings, but school libraries often have education code or administrative direction prohibiting this. This does not mean, however, that you need to abandon the idea of book sales altogether. Have your teachers, students, and parents clean off their bookshelves and donate their unwanted books to the library. You can hunt through the donations for items to add to the library collection and then offer the rest at a book sale.

Calendar

Organizing the printing and selling of a school calendar takes some advance planning. Getting advance sales is a good idea because it helps to figure out how many to print. Parents will want to purchase these if their child is in it in some fashion, such as a birthday calendar. You need only put the first name of the child and the grade since anonymity is essential. Parents and teachers will also purchase it for an easy place to refer to for school holidays, vacation days, testing periods, and events like back-to-school night and open house if those are on the calendar. The pictures for each month could feature school events or the students' favorite authors and books chosen (and permission sought) as a student literature and writing project.

Entertainment book

Entertainment books provide prospective customers with discounts for area restaurants and businesses.

Garden

If your school has a garden, you can grow flowers, plants, or produce that can be sold when harvested.

Guess the number

A large jar is filled with jellybeans or other small items. Participants pay to guess how many items are in the jar. At the end of the event, the guess closest to the correct amount wins the jar. This also works with pumpkins by guessing how many seeds are inside.

Holiday deliveries

Let students purchase fun goodies that will be delivered to their friends at school. Examples include Valentine roses, Halloween candy-grams, and St. Patrick's Day pencil-grams.

Library lollipops

Depending on your district's wellness policy, these may have to be sugar-free, but selling lollipops from a lollipop tree is a quick and easy way of raising funds all year long.

Merchandise

Check with your PTA's ways and means/fund-raising chairperson to find out about companies that work specifically with schools to help raise money. You will find a wide array of products that appeal to the general public.

Candles
Candy
Coffee and tea
Cookie dough
Flower bulbs
Gift wrap

Magazine subscriptions
Personalized keepsakes
Tree and seed kits

Trash and treasures or "white elephant" rummage sale

Have your supporters scavenge their closets, attics, and garages for unwanted items. They should know well in advance that they are donating these items and won't be receiving compensation. Don't bother with individually pricing anything, but you can group things in areas: $1 bins, $5 area, make an offer, etc. A really big, well-promoted sale will draw a crowd of Saturday- or Sunday-morning shoppers, and the early birds will arrive well before your stated start time. The original donations that are not sold will be given to charity.

School parking lot swap meet

Some housing tracts will choose a day for everyone in that area to share in advertising and hold a yard sale. If this is a new idea in your school area, and it is legally possible, choose one day and lease the spaces in your school parking lot and allow parents and teachers to sell their yard-sale items. Make sure to set up a food booth and play fun music. Please consider the area surrounding your school. If the parking lot is taken up with individuals selling their wares, where will the customers park?

Refreshments

Coordinate with other clubs and teams on campus to provide refreshment stands at their events.

Reusable shopping bags

Help reduce the use of plastic bags by creating environmentally friendly reusable cotton canvas bags that also carry the message about the importance of school libraries. They could also be used to carry books safely between home and school.

School supplies

While some schools may have bookstores, others do not and the school library is a good place to have machines that sell pencils and paper. Other school supplies such as notebooks and T-shirts are possible sales items if you have the space to store them and someone to handle sales when the "store" is open.

Pencils, pens, colored pencils, crayons, markers, highlighters
Erasers, pocket calculators, rulers, glue sticks, scissors, Post-it notes
Spiral notebooks, filler paper, journals, folders, binders
Printed school T-shirts, sweatshirts, jackets, caps

Events Held at Your School

Carnival/fair

An annual carnival, fair, or festival is a major fund-raising activity. Many months of planning and a huge cadre of volunteers are required to make the event a success. If another group is doing a large event like this, explore a way to earn funds with a booth.

Fall festival
Halloween haunt
Spring fling
End-of-the-year summer splash

Costume party
Have everyone dress up and offer prizes. Entry fee could be $20 or a brand-new book from your wish list.

Dances
Depending on your student and family population, there are a variety of dances that will provide a fun evening as well as money generated from ticket sales and refreshments.

Family dance
Father-daughter dance
Kids' dance
Retro dance (1970s, 1980s, or 1990s)
Sadie Hawkins Day
Sock hop
Sweetheart ball

Dessert
Having a dessert event is fun and quick. Usually you can do everything in less than two hours. You can ask local restaurants to provide mini-treats (let them distribute menus or coupons to generate new customers) and charge a small entrance fee to all that come. Another alternative is to buy all the fixings for sundaes and letting everyone make their own treats. Weigh the cup and charge a per-ounce fee.

Dinner
If you feed them, they will come. Common dinners are all-you-can-eat spaghetti, BBQ, and pizza. Theme events will generate interest, such as "The kids will make it for YOU!" and mystery-dinner theater.

Happy hour
Whether you call it a happy hour, social mixer, or early-bird eating, events held from 4 p.m. to 6 p.m. can generate a healthy profit.

Jail booth
Deputize your volunteers to work shifts at a local carnival, festival, or fair. People pay to have friends arrested and held for a short time, and arrestees can pay bail rather than wait to get out.

Karaoke night
Calling all singers . . . the cafeteria, school theater, or multipurpose room works well as a location. Have tables and chairs set up and rent or borrow a

karaoke machine. Have refreshments available for sale. Charge an entry fee and give a discount to those willing to sing to ensure there is entertainment. Allow people to sing solo or in groups. Having an emcee will keep things organized and music should play even if no one is stepping up to perform.

Make-believe beauty pageant

The sillier the contestants, the better, and make sure to invite plenty of male participants. You'll need a stage and seating for your audience, an emcee, and a witty script. Contestants should throw together wacky outfits and hairstyles. You won't have time to do much more than choose one competition. Depending on the group, you could have a talent portion, a question-and-answer session, or best evening dress. Audience participation or a panel of "celebrity" judges should choose the winner.

Outdoor film festival—movie night

Make sure you hold a public performance license or participate with Movie Licensing USA (http://www.movlic.com/) before showing the movie. The best venue depends on the weather and your space. You should be able to rent a giant outdoor screen or make one out of white sheets. You'll need a projector and speakers capable of allowing a big group sitting outside to hear. To hold it indoors, you'll need a large room, speakers, and a projection screen. You can charge a single price for the movie and refreshments or give one free with the purchase of the other, charge for each individually, or even charge nothing and simply ask for donations. Theme movie marathons are fun, and viewers should bring their sleeping bags and pillows for all-night events.

Pancake breakfast

You will need your school cafeteria, plenty of batter, and lots of volunteers. Put out signs and flyers well in advance of your event. Many of your local service organizations have this type of fund-raiser, and they might be willing to hold it to raise money for your library.

Sponsorship events

Participants get pledges from family and friends for a specific amount they will pay per lap/mile/page completed.

Book blitz—number of pages read or books read
Cycle (allow any kind: unicycles, bicycles, tricycles, Big Wheels, tandems, etc.)—number of laps on a track or number of miles on a course
Dance marathon—number of hours of uninterrupted dancing
Silence marathon—number of minutes a large group of children is able to keep completely silent
Sing—number of songs completed
Skip—can be done by time completed or laps/miles of skipping
Swim—number of lengths of the pool
Walk—number of laps or miles

Sometimes these events are called "a–thon." There are dozens, but here is a short list: read-a-thon, walk-a-thon, jog-a-thon, bike-a-thon, tricycle-a-thon, pogo stick-a-thon, hula hoop-a-thon, yo-yo-a-thon, jump rope-a-thon, sled-a-thon, dance-a-thon, bowl-a-thon, skate-a-thon, and cartwheel-a-thon.

Theme days

Students and teachers pay to participate (or for some teachers, it may be "pay to not participate") in a particular theme day at school. This could be a fancy dress-up day, wear jeans day, crazy hair day, temporary tattoo or face-painting day, or wear purple day.

1950s, 1960s, 1970s, 1980s, and 1990s nights

Sell tickets for a walk down memory lane night for parents and grandparents. Young and old can dress up in a particular era's outfits. Provide music from that era (DJ or band) along with drinks and food.

Events Off Campus

Bowling night

Regular bowling can be a lot of fun, and you can rent a bowling alley to do this, but there are a number of things you can do to make more money for the library. You can have something silly that has to be done on each frame, for example, throwing the ball granny-style, using the wrong hand, or bowling with your eyes closed. Have a few small prizes for the highest score; the first to get exactly 100 or best costumes if you encourage people to dress up. Check with the participating bowling alley to see if they have colored pins to use for "bowling for dollars" or crazy lights and music for cosmic bowling.

Restaurant night

Many restaurants offer nonprofit groups a way to raise money by giving them a percentage of sales on a designated night for all the customers that an organization brings to their business. Most of the time this will be one of their slow nights, and they may require customers to bring a flyer or coupon for their purchase to count toward the total. Many restaurants are independently owned and operated, so not every business on this list will hold these events, but they are good places to start. These include Applebee's, Big Boy, Chevy's Mexican Restaurants, Chili's, Fuddruckers, Outback Steakhouse, Panera Bread, Papa Murphy's, Pizzeria Uno, Ponderosa, and Souplantation & Sweet Tomatoes. Or just ask your local restaurant owner if it would be appropriate to participate.

Services

Car wash

Location is an important factor because you will want to find a place right off the main road that has water access. You'll need hoses, buckets, squeegees, wash towels, dry towels, sponges, and soap. You'll want plenty of poster-board signs and volunteers to help. You can charge a reasonable amount per car wash or call it "free" and let the car owners pay a donation.

Fast-food night
A variation of restaurant night, families eat at a designated fast-food restaurant on a specified night. Sometimes teachers and school staff work behind the counter taking orders, delivering food, or cleaning tables. The library receives a percentage of the sales during this time. Each franchise has its own program and rules, but restaurants that have advertised programs in the past include Arby's, Baja Fresh, Boston Market, Burger King, Carl's Jr., Chick-fil-A, Chipotle, Jack-in-the-Box, KFC, La Salsa, McDonald's, Pizza Hut, Rubio's, Sonic, Subway, and Wendy's.

Gift-wrap table
Work with stores or malls in coordination with holidays to provide gift-wrap service. You'll need to purchase the wrapping paper and have a large number of volunteers to keep it open during prime shopping hours.

Kids' tutorials
Parents often struggle to find tutoring for their child. Find students who are willing to tutor other students for free and have donations made to the library in their honor. Be sure to provide the library space for tutoring and keep track and celebrate students who give generously of their time.

Workshops or classes
If your school district allows it, you can offer workshops and classes in computer usage, research skills, Internet safety, or related topics for a fee that is earmarked for library programs.

Donations

Birthday book club

Parents donate money ($15 or the going price for a hardcover book) to the library in honor of their child during the month of the child's birthday. Having a special section of library for parents to choose from makes it easy for them to participate. Since the book is donated to the library, a bookplate is attached to the inside front cover stating it was donated by the child, who is given the option to be the first to check it out. To really get students excited about this program at the elementary level, wrap the book in birthday paper and have the child sit in your chair to open it and show the rest of the class during a visit.

Change boxes
Collect money by asking for donations of spare change. Think of a catchy theme and use coin-collection jars and containers that will remind everyone of your goal. Track classroom involvement and announce the results, as in a penny war.

Just ask for money
Simply ask for donations. You'd be surprised how many people are happier giving money directly to a good cause than if they have to purchase junk they don't want to give 10 cents on the dollar.

Letter-writing campaigns
Start by writing a great letter that everyone can personalize and send. Have anyone who is willing to participate fill out the envelope with their information on the return-address area because the recipient of the letter is more likely to open it. Make the case for friends and family to donate to the school library, and provide details about how the money will be spent and how it will help students and families. Use anecdotes and quotes from students about what it will mean to them. Include facts and figures about the current state of the library and provide a fund-raising goal. Include a pre-addressed return envelope to make it easy for donors to return it quickly and make sure it gets to the right place.

Pink flamingos
For this silly version of pay it forward, you'll need a good number of pink flamingos to begin. People who donate $20 get to choose a location for placing a flock of flamingos, generally in someone's yard or outside a business. A note is left explaining that the person or business has been selected by someone to be "flocked" for a good cause. Include directions so that the person/business flocked can pay $20 to have the flock removed. If the person/business doesn't respond within a predetermined time, remove the birds.

Quilt squares
If teachers and parents are donating for a specific cause, create a donor quilt acknowledging each donation and give it to the library.

Recognition
Major donations should be acknowledged in some meaningful, lasting way. Capital campaigns for major projects can benefit from the sale of personalized bricks or tiles or other similar items that will be near or inside the library to remind everyone of the contribution.

Recycling
Have students and teachers bring their aluminum and plastic to school. You'll need a large group of volunteers to help sort and bag the items and transport the bags (via truck) to a recycling center. There is also money to be made recycling printer cartridges and cell phones.

Web sites
Does your school library portal have a mechanism for people who would like to make online contributions? Talk to your information technology and fiscal services departments to make arrangements.

Contests

Adult spelling bee

Teachers and parents form teams of four. Each team pays an entry fee or gets sponsors. The spelling bee rules can be changed to tournament format with two teams going head to head and winning teams advancing to the next round. The winning team should get a trophy and bragging rights. Encourage the whole school to come out and watch.

Cook-off

Get competition going by having a chili cook-off, cake or cookie bake-off, or any kind of food-making contest where you can charge an entry fee for people to prove they are the best at making delicious food.

Kiss the pig

You might not want to use a pig due to concerns about swine flu, but a guinea pig or goat would work as well.

> Variation 1: If we meet our goal, the librarian (or principal) will kiss a pig at the next assembly.
>
> Variation 2: Students in each class donate change into one of two jars—either the "kiss the pig" jar or the "don't kiss the pig" jar. After the jars are counted, the one with more money is what the designated person has to do.

Mini-golf tournament

Find a location where you can lay out many different "holes," such as a practice field or playground. Have volunteer groups set up theme courses or holes on one large course and offer prizes for the best design and set-up. Borrow golf clubs to use as loaners. Families pay for and play the course as normal. This works best if it is a long event, perhaps six to eight hours, so that participants come and go. Issue staggered start times if you're worried about crowds and long waits.

Rubber-duck race

You will need to buy a lot of rubber ducks and get permission to use a local waterway that has a good current. Participants purchase the ducks (which should have stenciled numbers on their bottoms) for $5 to $20 each. All the ducks are dumped simultaneously into the water and the winning duck is the one that floats past the finish line first. The more ducks that are sold the better because the actual event will draw a large crowd to see 3,000 ducks floating down a stream! Alternatively, if you live in a landlocked area, you can use a pool where participants are given lanes and nets and a specified amount of time to see how many laps can be completed with the duck.

School "Idol"

Similar to the TV show *American Idol*, the teachers can be the judges and the pupils the performers, or vice versa. Charge friends and family an entry fee to watch the competition. This could also be done with a *So You Think You Can Dance* format.

Tournaments
Practically any game or sport can be played tournament style, with participants paying entry fees and spectators contributing to watch the competition. Examples of fun ones include three-on-three basketball, free-throws, golf, chess, Twister, darts, tennis, horseshoes, and lawn bowling.

Treasure hunt
Participants find clues, solve puzzles, or obtain objects on a set route. They are charged an entry fee for competing. They may also have to solve additional cryptic clues to identify objects and the order they saw along the route when they get to the final task. Depending on the type of hunt, the winner could be the first one to finish or the one who solves most clues or the one who collects the most items. This event can be organized to suit family teams or adults or children only.

Games of Chance

Cake walk

Find people willing to donate cakes that can be homemade or store bought. Put numbers on the ground, usually 1 through 20 (or more depending on how many participants you expect). Each person purchases a chance by paying a small fee (usually 25 to 50 cents) and standing on a number. Once all the numbers are taken, play music and have the participants walk around the circle of numbers. When the music stops, each person stands on the number they are nearest. A number is drawn at random and the person standing on that number wins the cake of their choice from the cake table.

Raffles
Get prizes donated for your raffle drawing well in advance of beginning sales. The better the prize, the more tickets you will be able to sell. Big-ticket items such as cars, travel packages, electronics like big-screen TVs, or gift certificates to places like Home Depot, Best Buy, or local restaurant chains will raise a lot of interest.

Air-band show or lip-synching contest
You'll need an auditorium, preferably with a stage, and a good sound system. Performers can be students, faculty, staff, or parents. Make sure you have a good emcee who will introduce each act and keep the show moving.

Concert
Whether you have a headline act, local bands, or school groups performing, a concert is a good way to raise funds. A large school campus can accommodate several stages so that audiences can rotate between them during set-up and break-down times. Make sure that you either provide seating or request

well in advance that ticket holders should bring chairs and/or blankets. See if you can find artists or groups who are willing to perform for free or at a very low cost. Find sponsors who will offset the cost of stages, speakers, and sound system, etc. Have food and drink booths set up, and offer them to other groups on campus for their fund-raisers. Their participation will bring more people to the concert.

Fashion show
Use administrators, teachers, parents, and/or students as models. Funds are raised through the selling of admission tickets, raffles, and possibly through the sale of clothes.

Magic show or talent show
Draw on the talents of your teacher friends and student performers, and get friends, parents, and teachers to come.

Singing telegrams
Enlist the help of your choir or just people who like to sing. Form singing teams of three or more, and assign each team a particular time to deliver singing cards. For each team, designate a captain who will be the spokesperson when the team arrives to sing for customers. Have them dress in unique costumes and take along goodies to hand out.

Appendix B: Station Teaching Examples

Creation station: Magazines, newspapers, and other art materials are provided for students to create a collage or poster to demonstrate what they know and learn about a topic of study

Expert groups: Students are split into teams and each team is expected to become expert on a topic, generally by meeting with the teacher to get explicit, small-group instruction. Teams are then let loose in the library to explore and discover more about the subject. Groups then share what they've learned with the other groups through presentations or sharing.

Genre studies: The school librarian gives instruction about the elements of a genre, then allows students to choose their own titles from a selection prepared by the librarian.

Partner reading: Selections are set out for students to read to each other and then have a discussion or debate about what is important or relevant.

Webquest: A guided inquiry on the computer that allows students to move at their own pace through a variety of resources chosen by the librarian. These resources can be text, video, simulations, or interactive activities, interspersed with assignments or quizzes.

Writing center: Materials and writing tools (dictionary, thesaurus, etc.) are provided to allow students to express themselves in writing.

Index

About the Author

JANICE GILMORE-SEE is the district librarian for La Mesa-Spring Valley School District, La Mesa, CA, overseeing 21 school-site libraries and the district instructional media center. She holds a bachelors degree in business information systems from the University of Phoenix and an MLIS from San Jose State University. She has written articles for *School Library Media Activities Monthly*, now *School Library Monthly*.